Detroit Studies in Music Bibliography

GENERAL EDITOR   BRUNO NETTL   UNIVERSITY OF ILLINOIS AT URBANA

Discography of Solo Song
SUPPLEMENT, 1975-1982

Dorothy Stahl

DETROIT STUDIES IN MUSIC BIBLIOGRAPHY   NUMBER FIFTY-TWO
INFORMATION COORDINATORS   1984   DETROIT

Copyright © 1984 by Dorothy Stahl

Printed and bound in the United States of America
Published by
Information Coordinators, Inc.
1435-37 Randolph Street
Detroit, Michigan 48226

Editing by J. Bunker Clark
Book design by Vincent Kibildis
Photocomposition by Elaine Gorzelski

Library of Congress Cataloging in Publication Data
Stahl, Dorothy.
A selected discography of solo song. Supplement, 1975-1982.
(Detroit studies in music bibliography ; no. 52)
Includes index.
1. Songs—Discography.
I. Title. II. Series: Detroit studies in music bibliography ; 52.
ML156.4.V7S8   1972   Suppl. 2   016.7899'1243   84-19794
ISBN 0-89990-023-2

Contents

Preface

This edition of *A Selected Discography of Solo Song* comprises recordings released since 1974. Previous editions in the Detroit Studies in Music Bibliography series are: *A Selected Discography of Solo Song,* no. 13 (1968; out of print) and its *Supplement, 1968-1969* (1970); *A Selected Discography of Solo Song: A Cumulation through 1971,* no. 24 (1972); and *A Selected Discography of Solo Song: Supplement, 1971-1974,* no. 34 (1976).

In the first section, the songs are arranged alphabetically by composer and under composer by title. Cycles are listed under the name of the cycle; when the songs are recorded separately, they are also entered under the title of the song with a reference to the complete cycle. Under the song title is the name of the artist, the title of the recording and the record number. Since many of the recordings consist of miscellaneous programs that include songs by various composers, each song is listed under the name of the composer.

The second section is a list of the releases indexed in the discography and includes the complete contents, the names of the artists in full and the record number. The first of this section's two parts consists of releases of the works of one composer in alphabetical order; the second, releases of works of two or more composers arranged alphabetically by record company, then numerically by serial number. The content of the records in each entry is alphabetical by title in the case of works of one composer. Anthologies are arranged alphabetically by composers and under composer by song title. Excerpts are followed by the title of the complete work in parentheses. In some cases, the recordings include compositions that are not within the scope of this index; these are not included in the main discography. This list may be used as a cross-reference with the discography where each title is listed under the name of the composer and which may include several recordings of the same work.

The third section is an index of song titles and first lines in one alphabetical listing.

Although there may be some recordings available which are not listed here, it is the intention of this discography to make accessible to teachers and students vocal works on recordings that can be easily procured.

DOROTHY STAHL

Smith College
Northampton, Massachusetts
August 1984

*R*ecord *L*abels with *A*bbreviations

Angel	Ang
Arabesque	Ara
Archive	Arch
Argo	
BIS	
Bruno Walter Society	BWS
Cambridge	Cam
CBS	
Caprice	
Cetra	
Claves	
Columbia	Col
Composers Recordings, Inc.	CRI
Connoisseur Society	Connoisseur
Decca	
Desmar	
Desto	

Deutsche Grammophon	DG
Discophilia	Disc
Eb-Sko	
Eclipse	
Electrola	EMI
Enigma	
Eurodisc	Euro
Everest	
Grenadilla	
Harmonia Mundi	HM
Helois	
HNH	
Hungaraton	Hung
Leonarda	
London	Lon
Metronome	Met
Musical Heritage Society	MHS
New World Records	NW
Nonesuch	None
Northeastern Records	NR
Odeon	
Odyssey	Ody
Oiseau-Lyre	Oiseau
Opus One	
Orion	
Pathé	
Pearl	
Pelican	Pel
Peters International	Peters
Philips	Phi
RCA	
Rococo	Roc
Saga	
Seraphim	Sera
Spectrum	
Telefunken	Tele
Unicorn	
Vanguard	Van

SECTION 1 *Discography of Solo Song*

Discography of Solo Song

ADAM, Charles (1803-56)
1 Mariquita
   Serate musicali. Joan Sutherland. Lon OSA-13132

AHROLD, Frank (b. 1931)
2 **Three Poems of Sylvia Plath** (Sheep in Fog; The Night Dances; Words)
   American Contemporary Words and Music. Corrine Curry. CRI SD 380

ALBENIZ, Isaac (1860-1909)
3 **Besa el aura**
4 **Del salón**
   Song Recital. Montserrat Caballé. Lon OS 26617
5 **Six Songs to Italian Texts** (Barcarola; La lontananza; Una rosa in dono;
   Il tuo sguardo; Morirò; T'ho riveduta in sogno)
   Recital. Victoria de los Angeles. Col M 35139

ALBERT, Stephen (b. 1941)
6 **To Wake the Dead** (How It Ends; Riverrun; Pray Your Prayers;
   Instruments; Forget, Remember; Sod's Brood, Mr. Finn; Passing Out)
   Music and Words. Sheila Marie Allen. CRI S-420

ANCHIETA, Juan de (1462-1523)
7 Con amores, la mi madre
   Canciones españolas. Teresa Berganza. DG 2530 598

APOSTEL, Hans-Erich (b. 1901)
8 Nacht
   Wirkung der neuen Wiener Schule im Lied. Dietrich Fischer-Dieskau.
   Odeon C 06502677

ARGENTO, Dominick (b. 1927)
9 Six Elizabethan Songs (Spring; Sleep; Winter; Dirge; Diaphenia; Hymn)
   American Contemporary Words and Music. Barbara Martin.
   CRI SD 380

AUBER, Daniel Francois Esprit (1782-1871)
10 L'Éclat de rire (Manon Lescaut)
   French Arias and Songs. Bidú Sayao. Ody Y 33130

AURIC, Georges (b. 1899)
11 **Alphabet** (Album; Bateau; Domino; Filet à papillons; Mallarmé; Hirondelle;
   Escarpin)
   Songs of Les Six. Maria Lagios. Spectrum SR-147
12 **Il était une petite pie**
13 **Les Pâquerettes**
14 **Une Petite Pomme**
15 **Les Petits Anes**
16 **La Poule noire**
17 **Printemps**
   Songs by Le Groupe des Six. Carole Bogard. Cam 2777

BABBITT, Milton (b. 1916)
18 **Philomel**
   Babbitt and Sessions. Bethany Beardslee. NW 307

BACH, Johann Sebastian (1685-1750)
19 **Ach, bleibe doch** (Cantata 11)
20 **Bereite dich, Zion** (Christmas Oratorio)
   Bach Arias. Janet Baker. Ang S-37229
21 **Bist du bei mir**
   Ein Liederabend. Elly Ameling. EMI C 063-02375
   Bach Arias. Janet Baker. Ang S-37229
   The Art of Elisabeth Schumann. Elisabeth Schumann. Sera 60320

22 **Er ist vollbracht** (St. John Passion)
23 **Et exultavit** (Magnificat in D Major)
24 **Gelobet sei der Herr** (Cantata 129)
25 **Hochgelobter Gottessohn** (Cantata 6)
26 **Komm, du süsse Todesstunde** (Cantata 161)
27 **Lobe, Zion, deinen Gott** (Cantata 190)
28 **Saget, saget mir geschwinde** (Easter Oratorio)
29 **Wohl euch ihr auserwählten Seelen** (Cantata 34)
   Bach Arias. Janet Baker. Ang S-37229

BÄCK, Sven-Erik (b. 1919)
30 **Neither Nor**
   Dorothy Dorow and Friends. Caprice RIKS LP 59

BACON, Ernst (b. 1898)
31 **The Banks of the Yellow Sea**
   American Songs. Carolyn Heafner. CRI SD 462
32 **Billy in the Darbies**
   An American Song Recital. William Parker. NW 305
33 **Eden**
34 **The Heart**
35 **I'm Nobody**
36 **Poor Little Heart**
37 **Simple Days**
   American Songs. Carolyn Heafner. CRI SD 462

BARAB, Seymour (b. 1921)
38 **Bits and Pieces** (Slow, Slow Fresh Fount; The Rain; Did Not; Waste; The Blossom; Late Riser; Do Not Love Too Long; There Was a King; I Heard a Linnet Courting)
   The Ariel Ensemble. Julia Lovett. Orion 81411

BARBER, Samuel (1910-81)
39 **I Hear an Army**
40 **Nocturne**
41 **A Nun Takes the Veil**
42 **Rain Has Fallen**
43 **The Secrets of the Old**
44 **Sleep Now**
45 **Solitary Hotel**
   Joan Patenaude. MHS 3770

15

BARBER, Samuel—*continued*
46 Sure on This Shining Night
   But Yesterday Is Not Today. Bethany Beardslee. NW 243
   Joan Patenaude. MHS 3770
47 With Rue My Heart Is Laden
   Joan Patenaude. MHS 3770

BARTÓK, Béla (1881-1945)
48 Im Tale
   Aufbruch des 20. Jahrhunderts im Lied. Dietrich Fischer-Dieskau.
   Odeon C 06502676

BAUR, John (b. 1947)
49 The Moon and the Yew Trees
   Voices and Instruments. Christine Anderson. CRI SD 426

BAUTISTA, Julian (1901-61)
50 Three Songs Dedicated to Andalusian Cities (Malaguena; Barrio de
   Córdoba; Baile)
   Recital. Victoria de los Angeles. Col M 35139

BEACH, Amy Marcy Cheney (Mrs. H. H. A.) (1867-1944)
51 Ah, Love, But a Day
52 I Send My Heart Up to Thee
53 The Year's at the Spring
   American Songs. Carolyn Heafner. CRI SD 462

BECK, Conrad (b. 1901)
54 Herbst
   Wirkung der neuen Wiener Schule im Lied. Dietrich Fischer-Dieskau.
   Odeon C 06502677

BEDFORD, David (b. 1937)
55 Music for Albion Moonlight (So It Ends; If We Are To Know Where
   We Live; Lament for the Makers of Songs; Fall of the Evening Star)
   Lutyens-Bedford. Jane Manning. Argo ZRG 638

BEESON, Jack (b. 1921)
56 Death by Owl-Eyes
57 Eldorado
58 The You Should Of Done It Blues
   American Songs. Carolyn Heafner. CRI SD 462

16

BEETHOVEN, Ludwig van (1770-1827)

59 An Laura
60 Das Blümchen Wunderhold
    Beethoven Lieder. Max van Egmond. Met MPS 168,004
61 Bonny Laddie
    Scottish Folk Songs. Janet Baker. Ang S-37172
62 The British Light Dragoons
    Folksongs. Robert White. RCA ARLI-3417
63 Cease Your Funning
    Scottish Folk Songs. Janet Baker. Ang S-37172
    Folksongs. Robert White. RCA ARLI-3417
64 Come Draw We Round the Cheerful Ring
65 Cupid's Kindness
    Folksongs. Robert White. RCA ARLI-3417
66 Elegie auf den Tod eines Pudels
    Beethoven Lieder. Max van Egmond. Met MPS 168,004
67 Faithfu' Johnie
    Scottish Folk Songs. Janet Baker. Ang S-37172
68 Feuerfarb
    Beethoven Lieder. Max van Egmond. Met MPS 168,004
69 Good Night
70 The Kiss, Dear Maid, Thy Lip Has Left
    Folksongs. Robert White. RCA ARLI-3417
71 Klage
72 Lied
73 Das Liedchen von der Ruhe
74 Mailied
75 Marmotte
    Beethoven Lieder. Max van Egmond. Met MPS 168,004
76 O Harp of Erin
77 O Mary, at Thy Window Be
78 On the Massacre of Glencoe
79 The Pulse of an Irishman
80 The Return to Ulster
81 Sally in Our Alley
    Folksongs. Robert White. RCA ARLI-3417
82 Selbstgespräch
    Beethoven Lieder. Max van Egmond. Met MPS 168,004
83 The Sweetest Lad Was Jamie
    Scottish Folk Songs. Janet Baker. Ang S-37172
84 The Soldier
85 'Tis Sunshine at Last
    Folksongs. Robert White. RCA ARLI-3417

BEETHOVEN, Ludwig van—*continued*
86 Urians Reise um die Welt
   Beethoven Lieder. Max van Egmond. Met MPS 168,004
87 The Vale of Clwyd
88 When Mortals All to Rest Retire
   Folksongs. Robert White. RCA ARLI-3417
89 Wonne der Wehmut
   Ein Liederabend. Elly Ameling. EMI 063-02375

BELL, Daniel (b. 1928)
90 Grass
   Dorothy Dorow and Friends. Caprice RIKS LP 59

BELLINI, Vincenzo (1801-35)
91 Bella Nice che d'amore
   Pavarotti in Concert. Luciano Pavarotti. Lon OS-26391
92 Che inargenti
   Serate musicali. Joan Sutherland. Lon OSA-13132
93 Dolente immagine di fille mia
   Recital. Leyla Gencer. Cetra LPO 2003
   Pavarotti in Concert. Luciano Pavarotti. Lon OS-26391
   Songs. Renata Scotto. RCA V-AGLI 1-1341
   Serate musicali. Joan Sutherland. Lon OSA-13132
   Recital of Songs and Arias. Renata Tebaldi. Lon R 23219
94 Il fervido desiderio
   Portrayals of Love in Italian Song. Anna Gabrieli. Orion ORS-78307
   Recital. Leyla Gencer. Cetra LPO 2003
95 Malinconia ninfa gentile
   Pavarotti in Concert. Luciano Pavarotti. Lon OS-26391
   Songs. Renata Scotto. RCA V-AGLI 1-1341
   Serate musicali. Joan Sutherland. Lon OSA-13132
96 Ma rendi pur contento
   Pavarotti in Concert. Luciano Pavarotti. Lon OS-26391
97 Per pieta bell'idol mio
   Songs. Renata Scotto. RCA V-AGLI 1-1341
98 Vaga luna che inargenti
   Portrayals of Love in Italian Song. Anna Gabrieli. Orion ORS-78307
   Recital. Leyla Gencer. Cetra LPO 2003
   Songs. Renata Scotto. RCA V-AGLI 1-1341
   Serate musicali. Joan Sutherland. Lon OSA-13132
99 Vanne, O rosa fortunata
   Pavarotti in Concert. Luciano Pavarotti. Lon OS-26391
   Recital of Songs and Arias. Renata Tebaldi. Lon R 23219

BENNETT, Richard Rodney (b. 1936)
100 Tom O'Bedlams Song
Twentieth Century English Songs. Peter Pears. Argo ZRG 5418
English Songs. Peter Pears. Argo ZK 28-29

BERG, Alban (1885-1935)
101 Seven Early Songs (Nacht; Schilflied; Die Nachtigall; Traumgekrönt;
Im Zimmer; Liebesode; Sommertage)
Joan Patenaude. MHS 3770

BERGER, Jean (b. 1909)
102 Cinq Chansons *(Mary Stuart)* (Pour lui j'ay méprise l'honneur; Car c'est le
seul désir; Sans cesse mon coeur; Vous m'éstimez légère; O Domine Deus)
Mélodies. Carol Kimball. Orion ORS-82422

BERGER, Ludwig (1777-1839)
103 Trost in Tränen
German Romantic Songs. Karl Markus. MHS 1962

BERKELEY, Lennox (b. 1903)
104 How Love Came In
An English Song Recital. Peter Pears. Eclipse ECS 545

BERLIOZ, Hector (1803-69)
105 Auf den Lagunen
Lieder der Neudeutschen. Dietrich Fischer-Dieskau. Odeon
C 06502674
106 La Belle Voyageuse
107 Le Coucher du soleil
A Recital of French Songs. Jill Gomez. Saga 5388
108 Les Nuits d'été (Villanelle; Le Spectre de la rose; Sur les lagunes;
L'Absence; Au cimitière; L'Île inconnue)
Berlioz and Ravel. Jessye Norman. Phi 9500 783
109 L'Origine de la harpe
A Recital of French Songs. Jill Gomez. Saga 5388

BIZET, Georges (1838-75)
110 Adieux de l'hôtesse Arabe
A Recital of French Songs. Jill Gomez. Saga 5388
111 Berceuse
Songs. Carole Bogard. Cam CRS-2775

BIZET, Georges—*continued*
  112 **Chanson d'avril**
   Songs. Carole Bogard. Cam CRS-2775
   A Recital of French Songs. Jill Gomez. Saga 5388
   Reynaldo Hahn and His Songs. Reynaldo Hahn. Roc 5365
  113 **La Chanson de la rose**
   A Recital of French Songs. Jill Gomez. Saga 5388
  114 **Chant d'amour**
   Songs. Carole Bogard. Cam CRS-2775
  115 **Ouvre ton coeur**
   Plaisir d'amour. Beverly Sills. Col M-33933
  116 **Pastorale**
   Serate musicale. Joan Sutherland. Lon OSA-13132
  117 **Vous ne priez pas**
   A Recital of French Songs. Jill Gomez. Saga 5388

BLACHER, Boris (1903-75)
  118 **Aprèslude** (Gedicht; Worte)
   Aufbruch des 20. Jahrhunderts im Lied. Dietrich Fischer-Dieskau.
   Odeon C 06502676
  119 **Francesca di Rimini, op. 47**
   Music for Voice and Violin. Catherine Malfitano. MHS 1976

BLANK, Allan (b. 1925)
  120 **Two Songs for Voice and Bassoon** (Don't Let That Horse Eat That
   Violin; The Pennycandystore Beyond the El)
   Other Voices. Jan De Gaetani. CRI SD 370

BONONCINI, Antonio Maria (1677-1726)
  121 **Deh più a me non v'ascondete**
   Arie amorose. Janet Baker. Phi 9500 557
   Eighteenth Century Arias. Renata Tebaldi. Lon OS 26376
  122 **Per la gloria**
   Pavarotti in Concert. Luciano Pavarotti. Lon OS-26391

BOULANGER, Lili (1893-1918)
  123 **Clairières dans le ciel** (Elle était descendue; Elle est gravement gaie;
   Parfois, je suis triste; Un Poète disait; Au pied de mon lit; Si tout ceci
   n'est qu'un pauvre rêve; Vous m'avez regardé avec toute votre âme;
   Nous nous aimerons tant; Les Lilas qui avaient fleuri; Deux Ancolies;
   Par ce que j'ai souffert; Je garde une médaille d'elle; Demain fera un an)
   Songs of Lili Boulanger. Paulina Stark. Spectrum UNI-PRO SR-126

BOWLES, Paul (b. 1911)
124 Once a Lady Was Here
125 Song of an Old Woman
   But Yesterday Is Not Today. Donald Gramm. NW 243

BRAHMS, Johannes (1833-97)
126 Agnes, op. 59/5
   Brahms Lieder. Elly Ameling. Phi 9500 398
127 Alto Rhapsody, op. 53
   Concert. Janet Baker. Ang SQ-37199
128 Auf dem Kirchhofe, op. 105/4
   Brahms Lieder. Janet Baker. Ang S-37519
   German Songs. Benita Valente. Desmar DSM 1010
129 Blinde Kuh
   To My Friends. Elisabeth Schwarzkopf. Lon OS 26592
130 Botschaft, op. 47/1
   Brahms Lieder. Elly Ameling. Phi 9500 398
   Schubert and Brahms Lieder. Marian Anderson. RCA ARLI-3022
   Brahms Lieder. Jessye Norman. Phi 9500 785
131 Da unten im Tale
   Ein Liederabend. Elly Ameling. EMI 063-02375
132 Dein blaues Augen, op. 59/8
   Brahms Lieder. Elly Ameling. Phi 9500 398
   Schubert and Brahms Lieder. Marian Anderson. RCA ARLI-3022
   Lieder Recital. Julia Hamari. Hung SLPX-12406
133 Des Liebsten Schwur, op. 69/4
   Brahms Lieder. Elly Ameling. Phi 9500 398
134 Feldeinsamkeit, op. 86/2
   An Evening of Brahms Songs. Christa Ludwig. Col M-34535
135 Der Frühling, op. 6/2
   Brahms Lieder. Elly Ameling. Phi 9500 398
136 Der Ganz zur Liebchen
   Recital. Elena Gerhardt. Disc KG-G-4
137 Geistliches Wiegenlied, op. 91 (with viola)
138 Gestille Sehnsucht, op. 91 (with viola)
   Brahms Lieder. Janet Baker. Ang S-37519
   Brahms Lieder. Jessye Norman. Phi 9500 785
139 Heimweh, op. 63/8
   Brahms Lieder. Elly Ameling. Phi 9500 398
140 Immer leiser wird mein Schlummer, op. 105/2
   Brahms Lieder. Elly Ameling. Phi 9500 398
   An Evening of Brahms Songs. Christa Ludwig. Col M-34535
   Brahms Lieder. Jessye Norman. Phi 9500 785

BRAHMS, Johannes *—continued*

141 **In den Beeren,** op. 84/3
    Brahms Lieder Elly Ameling. Phi 9500 398
142 **Der Jäger,** op. 95/4
    Brahms Lieder. Elly Ameling. Phi 9500 398
    Brahms Lieder. Janet Baker. Ang S-37519
143 **Komm bald,** op. 97/5
    Brahms Lieder. Elly Ameling. Phi 9500 398
144 **Liebestreu,** op. 3/1
    De los Angeles in Concert. Victoria de los Angeles. Ang SZ-37546
    An Evening of Brahms Songs. Christa Ludwig. Col M-34535
145 **Mädchenlied,** op. 107/5
    An Evening of Brahms Songs. Christa Ludwig. Col M-34535
    To My Friends. Elisabeth Schwarzkopf. Lon OS 26592
146 **Das Mädchen spricht,** op. 107/3
    Brahms Lieder. Elly Ameling. Phi 9500 398
147 **Die Mainacht,** op. 43/2
    An Evening of Brahms Songs. Christa Ludwig. Col M-34535
    Brahms Lieder. Jessye Norman. Phi 9500 785
148 **Meine Liebe ist grün,** op. 63/5
    Brahms Lieder. Jessye Norman. Phi 9500 785
    German Songs. Benita Valente. Desmar DSM 1010
149 **Mein Mädel hat einen Rosenmund**
    Think on Me. Elly Ameling. CBS 36682
150 **Nachtigall,** op. 97/1
    The Art of Elisabeth Schumann. Elisabeth Schumann. Sera 60320
    German Songs. Benita Valente. Desmar DSM 1010
151 **Och Moder, ich well en Ding han**
    German Romantic Songs. Elly Ameling. Phi 9500 350
152 **O komme, holde Sommernacht,** op. 58/4
    Brahms Lieder. Jessye Norman. Phi 9500 785
153 **Regenlied,** op. 59/3
    Brahms Lieder. Janet Baker. Ang S-37519
154 **Ruhe, süssliebchen, im Schatten,** op. 33/9
    An Evening of Brahms Songs. Christa Ludwig. Col M-34535
155 **Sandmännchen**
    Brahms Lieder. Elly Ameling. Phi 9500 398
156 **Sapphische Ode,** op. 94/4
    Brahms Lieder. Janet Baker. Ang S-37519
    An Evening of Brahms Songs. Christa Ludwig. Col M-34535
157 **Der Schmied,** op. 19/4
    Schubert and Brahms Lieder. Marian Anderson. RCA ARLI-3022

158 **Schwesterlein**
    German Romantic Songs. Elly Ameling. Phi 9500 350
159 **Spanisches Lied,** op. 6/1
    Brahms Lieder. Elly Ameling. Phi 9500 398
160 **Ständchen,** op. 106/1
    Brahms Lieder. Janet Baker. Ang S-37519
    Lieder Recital. Julia Hamari. Hung SLPX-12406
    An Evening of Brahms Songs. Christa Ludwig. Col M-34535
    Brahms Lieder. Jessye Norman. Phi 9500 785
161 **Therese,** op. 86/1
    Brahms Lieder. Janet Baker. Ang S-37519
    Recital. Elena Gerhardt. Disc KG-G-4
    Brahms Lieder. Jessye Norman. Phi 9500 785
    To My Friends. Elisabeth Schwarzkopf. Lon OS 26592
    German Songs. Benita Valente. Desmar DSM 1010
162 **Der Tod, das ist die kühle Nacht,** op. 96/1
    Recital. Elena Gerhardt. Disc KG-G-4
    An Evening of Brahms Songs. Christa Ludwig. Col M-34535
    Brahms Lieder. Jessye Norman. Phi 9500 785
    German Songs. Benita Valente. Desmar DSM 1010
163 **Die Trauernde,** op. 7/5
    Brahms Lieder. Elly Ameling. Phi 9500 398
164 **Vergebliches Ständchen,** op. 84/4
    Brahms Lieder. Elly Ameling. Phi 9500 398
    Schubert and Brahms Lieder. Marian Anderson. RCA ARLI-3022
    Brahms Lieder. Janet Baker. Ang S-37519
    Victoria de los Angeles in Concert. Ang SZ-37546
    German Songs. Benita Valente. Desmar DSM 1010
165 **Vier ernste Gesänge,** op. 121 (Denn es gehet dem Menschen; Ich
    wandte mich; O Tod, wie bitter; Wenn ich mit Menschen)
    Brahms Lieder. Janet Baker. Ang S-37519
166 **Von ewiger Liebe,** op. 43/1
    Brahms Lieder. Elly Ameling. Phi 9500 398
    Schubert and Brahms Lieder. Marian Anderson. RCA ARLI-3022
    An Evening of Brahms Songs. Christa Ludwig. Col M-34535
    Brahms Lieder. Jessye Norman. Phi 9500 785
167 **Von Waldbekränzter Höhe,** op. 57/1
168 **Wiegenlied,** op. 49/4
    Brahms Lieder. Elly Ameling. Phi 9500 398
169 **Wie Melodien zieht es mir,** op. 105/1
    Brahms Lieder. Janet Baker. Ang S-37519
    Brahms Lieder. Jessye Norman. Phi 9500 785

BRAHMS, Johannes—*continued*
170 **Zigeunerlieder,** op. 103 (He, Zigeuner; Hochgetürmte Rimaflut; Wisst ihr, wann mein Kindchen; Lieber Gott, du weisst; Brauner Bursche führt zum Tanze; Röslein dreie; Kommt dir manchmal in den Sinn; Rote Abendwolken)
Recital. Elena Gerhardt. Disc KG-G-4
An Evening of Brahms Songs. Christa Ludwig. Col M-34535

BRIDGE, Frank (1879-1941)
171 **Goldenhair**
English Songs. Peter Pears. Argo ZK 28-29
Twentieth Century English Songs. Peter Pears. Argo ZRG 5418
172 **Go Not, Happy Day**
An English Song Recital. Peter Pears. Eclipse ECS 545
173 **Journey's End**
English Songs. Peter Pears. Argo ZK 28-29
Twentieth Century English Songs. Peter Pears. Argo ZRG 5418
174 **Love Went A-Riding**
An English Songs Recital. Peter Pears. Eclipse ECS 545
175 **So Perverse**
176 **'Tis But a Week**
177 **When You Are Old**
English Songs. Peter Pears. Argo ZK 28-29
Twentieth Century English Songs. Peter Pears. Argo ZRG 5418

BRITTEN, Benjamin (1913-76)
178 **The Ash Grove**
Britten Songs. Bernadette Greevy. London STS-15166
179 **A Birthday Hansel,** op. 92 (Birthday Song; My Early Walk; Wee Willie; My Hoggie; Afton Water; The Winter; Leezie Lindsay)
Benjamin Britten. Peter Pears. Lon SR 33257
180 **The Bonny Earl of Moray**
Britten Songs. Bernadette Greevy. London STS-15166
181 **Canticle V—The Death of Saint Narcissus**
182 **Ca' the Yowes**
Benjamin Britten. Peter Pears. Lon SR 33257
183 **A Charm of Lullabies,** op. 41 (A Cradle Song; The Highland Balou; Sephestia's Lullaby; A Charm; The Nurse's Song)
184 **Come You Not from Newcastle?**
Britten Songs. Bernadette Greevy. Lon STS-15166
185 **French Folk Song Arrangements** (La Noël passée; Le Roi s'en va-t'en chasse; Il est quelqu'un sur terre; Eho! Eho!; Quand j'étais chez mon père)

An Album of French Songs. Martial Singher. 1750 Arch S-1766

186 **I Will Give My Love an Apple**
   Music for Voice and Guitar. Peter Pears. RCA AGLI-1281

187 **Let the Florid Music Praise**
   An English Song Recital. Peter Pears. Eclipse ECS 545

188 **Master Kilby**
   Music for Voice and Guitar. Peter Pears. RCA AGLI-1281

189 **O Can Ye Sew Cushions?**
   Britten Songs. Bernadette Greevy. Lon STS-15166
   Benjamin Britten. Peter Pears. Lon SR 33257

190 **Oliver Cromwell**
   Britten Songs. Bernadette Greevy. Lon STS-15166

191 **O Waly, Waly**
   Souvenirs. Elly Ameling. Col M 35119
   Britten Songs. Bernadette Greevy. Lon STS-15166

192 **Sailor-Boy**
   Music for Voice and Guitar. Peter Pears. RCA AGLI-1281

193 **The Salley Gardens**
   Britten Songs. Bernadette Greevy. Lon STS-15166

194 **Second Lute Song** from *Gloriana*
   Benjamin Britten. Peter Pears. Lon SR 33257
   Music for Voice and Guitar. Peter Pears. RCA AGLI-1281

195 **The Shooting of His Dear**

196 **The Soldier and the Sailor**

197 **Songs from the Chinese** (The Big Chariot; The Old Lute; The Autumn
   Wind; The Herd-Boy; Depression; Dance Song)
   Music for Voice and Guitar. Peter Pears. RCA AGLI-1281

198 **Sweet Polly Oliver**

199 **There's None to Sooth**
   Britten Songs. Bernadette Greevy. Lon STS-15166

200 **Tit for Tat** (A Song of Enchantment; Autumn; Silver; Vigil; Tit for Tat)
   Britten and Purcell. John Shirley-Quirk. Decca SXL 6608

201 **The Trees They Grow So High**
   Britten Songs. Bernadette Greevy. Lon STS-15166

202 **Who Are These Children?**, op. 84 (A Riddle; A Laddie's Sang;
   Nightmare; Black Day; Bed-Time; Slaughter; A Riddle; The Larky Lad;
   Who Are These Children?; Supper; The Children; The Auld Aik)
   Britten and Purcell. Peter Pears. Decca SXL 6608

203 **Winter Words**, op. 52 (At Day Close in November; Midnight on the Great
   Western; Wagtail and Baby; The Little Old Table; The Choirmaster's
   Burial; Proud Songsters; Before Life and After)
   An Album of English Songs. Ian Partridge. MHS 4531

BUSCH, William (1901-45)
204 Come, O Come, My Life's Delight
205 The Echoing Green
206 If Thou Wilt Ease Thine Heart
207 The Shepherd
    English Songs. Peter Pears. Argo ZK 28-29

BUSH, Geoffrey (b. 1920)
208 Echo's Lament for Narcissus
    An Album of English Songs. Ian Partridge. MHS 4531
209 Voices of the Prophets (From Isaiah; Milton; Blake; Blackman)
    English Songs. Peter Pears. Argo ZK 28-29
210 The Wonder of Wonders
    An Album of English Songs. Ian Partridge. MHS 4531

BUTTERWORTH, George (1885-1916)
211 Is My Team Ploughing?
    An English Song Recital. Peter Pears. Eclipse ECS 545

CACCINI, Giulio (ca. 1545-1618)
212 Amarilli, mia bella
    Arie amorose. Janet Baker. Phi 9500 557

CALDARA, Antonio (1670-1736)
213 Come raggio di sol
    Arie amorose. Janet Baker. Phi 9500 557
    Italian Baroque Songs. Teresa Berganza. DG 2531 192
214 Sebben crudele
    Arie amorose. Janet Baker. Phi 9500 557
215 Selve amiche
    Arie amorose. Janet Baker. Phi 9500 557
    Italian Baroque Songs. Teresa Berganza. DG 2531 192
216 Vaghe luci
    Songs of the Italian Baroque. Carlo Berganzi. HNH 4008

CAMPANA, Fabio (1815-82)
217 L'ultime speme
    Serate musicali. Joan Sutherland. Lon OSA-13132

CAMPRA, Andre (1660-1744)
218 Chanson du papillon (*Les Fêtes venitiennes*)
    French Arias and Songs. Bidú Sayao. Ody Y33130

CANTELOUBE, Joseph (1879-1957)
219 L'aïo de rotso
    Von Stade Live. Frederica Von Stade. Col IM-37231
220 Brezairola
    Souvenirs. Elly Ameling. Col M-35119
    Von Stade Live. Frederica Von Stade. Col IM-37231
221 Chants de France (Auprès de ma blonde; Ou irai-je me plaindre?; Au pré de la rose; D'ou venez-vous, fillette?)
    Von Stade Live. Frederica Von Stade. Col IM-37231

CARISSIMI, Giacomo (1605-76)
222 Amor mie, che cosa è questo?
223 Apritevi, Inferni
224 Bel tempo per me se n'andò
225 Deh, memoria
226 In un mar di pensieri
227 No no mio core
    Carissimi Cantatas. Martyn Hill. Oiseau DSLO 547
228 No, non si speri
    Italian Baroque Songs. Teresa Berganza. DG 2531 192
229 Suonerà l'ultima tromba
230 V'intendo, v'intendo occhi
    Carissimi Cantatas. Martyn Hill. Oiseau DSLO 547
231 Vittoria, mio cuore
    Italian Baroque Songs. Teresa Berganza. DG 2531 192

CARPENTER, John Alden (1876-1951)
232 Gitanjali (When I Bring to You Coloured Toys; On the Day When Death Will Knock at Thy Door; The Sleep That Flits on Baby's Eyes; I Am Like a Remnant of a Cloud of Autumn; On the Seashore of Endless Worlds; Light, My Light)
    Songs. Alexandra Hunt. Orion 77272

CATALANI, Alfredo (1854-93)
233 La notte è placida
234 Vieni! deh, vien
    Serenata. Renata Scotto. Col M-34501

CAVALLI, Pier Francesco (1602-76)
235 Son ancor pargoletta
    Italian Baroque Songs. Teresa Berganza. DG 2531 192

CESTI, Marcantonio (1618-69)
236 Intorno all'idol mio
   Arie amorose. Janet Baker. Phi 9500 557

CHABRIER, Alexis Emanuel (1841-94)
237 Ballade des Gros Dindons
238 Chanson pour Jeanne
   Chabrier and Liszt. Paul Sperry. Orion ORS 75174
239 Les Cigales
   Reynaldo Hahn and His Songs. Reynaldo Hahn. Roc 5365
   Chabrier and Liszt. Paul Sperry. Orion ORS 75174
240 L'Île heureuse
   Songs. Carole Bogard. Cam CRS-2775
   Reynaldo Hahn and His Songs. Reynaldo Hahn. Roc 5365
   Chabrier and Liszt. Paul Sperry. Orion ORS 75174
241 Lied
   Songs. Carole Bogard. Cam CRS-2775
   Chabrier and Liszt. Paul Sperry. Orion ORS 75174
242 Pastorale des petits cochons roses
   Chabrier and Liszt. Paul Sperry. Orion ORS 75174
243 Toutes les fleurs
   Reynaldo Hahn and His Songs. Reynaldo Hahn. Roc 5365
244 Villanelle des petits canards
   Chabrier and Liszt. Paul Sperry. Orion ORS 75174

CHAMINADE, Cécile (1857-1944)
245 Berceuse
   Serate musicali. Joan Sutherland. Lon OSA-13132

CHANLER, Theodore (1902-61)
246 The Children
   But Yesterday Is Not Today. Donald Gramm. NW 243
247 Four Rhymes from "Peacock Pie" (The Ship of Rio; Old Shellover;
   Cake and Sack; Tillie)
   Anthology of American Music. William Parker. NW 300
248 Moo Is a Cow (*The Children*)
249 Once Upon a Time (*The Children*)
250 The Rose (*The Children*)
   But Yesterday Is Not Today. Donald Gramm. NW 243
251 These, My Ophelia
   But Yesterday Is Not Today. Bethany Beardslee. NW 243
252 Thomas Logge
   But Yesterday Is Not Today. Donald Gramm. NW 243

CHAUSSON, Ernest (1855-99)
253 Amour d'antan, op. 8/2
254 La Caravane, op. 14
255 Le Charme, op. 2/2
    Songs. Jan De Gaetani. None H-71373
256 Le Colibri, op. 2/7
257 Les Papillons, op. 2/3
    Ein Liederabend. Elly Ameling. EMI 063-02375
    Songs. Jan De Gaetani. None H-71373
    An Album of French Songs. Martial Singher. 1750 Arch S-1766
258 Poème de l'amour et de la mer, op. 19 (La Fleur des eaux; Interlude;
    La Mort de l'amour; Le Temps des lilas)
    Chausson and Duparc. Janet Baker. Ang S-37401
259 Le Temps des lilas, op. 19. *See also* 258
    Chausson and Duparc. Janet Baker. Ang S-27401
    Songs. Jan De Gaetani. None H-71373
    An Album of French Songs. Martial Singher. 1750 Arch S-1766

CHOPIN, Frederic (1810-49)
260 Melodie polacche (Desiderio di fanciolla; Ballata; Primavera; Il guerrioro)
    Recital. Leyle Gencer. Cetra LPO 2003. *See also* 261
261 Seventeen Polish Songs, op. 74 (The Maiden's Wish; In Spring; Troubled
    Waters; Bacchanal; What a Young Maiden Loves; Go Thou, and Haste
    Thee; The Messenger; My Sweetheart; A Melody; The Trooper Before
    the Battle; Two Corpses; My Joys; Melancholy; The Little Ring; The
    Return Home; Lithuanian Song; Poland's Dirge)
    Chopin Songs. Annette Celine. Everest 3370
    Eugenia Zareska. Helois H-88001
262 Two Posthumous Songs (Charms; Reverie)
    Chopin Songs. Annette Celine. Everest 3370
263 Tristesse. *See also* 261
    French Arias and Songs. Bidú Sayao. Ody Y33130

CIMARA, Pietro (1887-1967)
264 Stornello
    Serate musicali. Joan Sutherland. Lon OSA-13132

CITKOWITZ, Israel (1909-74)
265 Five Songs from "Chamber Music" (Strings in the Earth and Air;
    When the Shy Star Goes Forth in Heaven; O, It Was Out by
    Donnycarney; Bid Adieu, Adieu, Adieu; My Love Is in a Light Attire)
    But Yesterday Is Not Today. Bethany Beardslee. NW 243

CLÉRAMBAULT, Louis Nicolas (1676-1749)
266 Médée
267 Orphée
Rachel Yakar. Arch 2533 442

COPLAND, Aaron (b. 1900)
268 Song
But Yesterday Is Not Today. Bethany Beardslee. NW 243
269 **Why Do They Shut Me Out of Heaven?** (*Poems of Emily Dickinson*)
Von Stade Live. Frederica Von Stade. Col IM-37231

CORNELIUS, Peter (1824-74)
270 Liebe ohne Heimat
271 Sonnenuntergang
Lieder der Neudeutschen. Dietrich Fischer-Dieskau. Odeon
C 06502674
272 Ein Ton
273 Wiegenlied
Farewell Recital. Lotte Lehman. Pel LP 2009

COSTANZI, Giovanni Battista (1704-78)
274 Lusinga la speme (*Eupatra*)
Arie antiche. Montserrat Caballé. Lon OS 26618

DALAYRAC, Nicholas (1753-1809)
275 Quand le bienaimé reviendra
Serate musicali. Joan Sutherland. Lon OSA-13132

DALLAPICCOLA, Luigi (1904-75)
276 **Cinque canti** (Aspettiamo la stella; Dorati uccelli dall'acuta voce;
Acheronte che tormenti reca; Dormono le cime dei monti; Ardano,
attraverso la notte)
The Music of Dallapiccola. Tom Buckner. 1750 Arch 1782
277 **Divertimento in quattro esercizi** (Non mi mandar messaggi; E per il bel
d'un merlo; L'acqua corre alla borrana; Mamma, lo temp'è venuto)
278 **Quattro liriche di Antonio Machado** (La primavera ha venido; Ayer soné
que veia; Senor, ya me arrancaste; La primavera ha venido)
The Music of Dallapiccola. Anna Carol Dudley. 1750 Arch 1782
279 **Rencesvals**
The Music of Dallapiccola. Tom Buckner. 1750 Arch 1782

280 **Sieben Goethe-Lieder** (In tausend Forman magst du dich verstecken;
Die Sonne kommt; Lass deinen süssen Robinenmund; Möge Wasser,
springend, wallend; Der Spiegel sagt mir, ich bin schön; Kaum, dass
ich dich wieder habe; Ist's möglich, dass ich Liebchen dich kose)
Lieder. Dorothy Dorow. Tele 6/42350 AW

DAVID, Felicien (1810-76)
281 **Les Hirondelles**
Serate musicali. Joan Sutherland. Lon OSA-13132

DAVIES, Peter Maxwell (b. 1934)
282 **Dark Angels** (The Drowning Brothers; Dark Angels [guitar solo];
Dead Fires)
Davies and Wernick. Jan De Gaetani. None H-71342

DEBUSSY, Claude (1862-1918)
283 **Aimon-nous et dormons**
Mélodies françaises. Mady Mesplé. Odeon 2C 069-14089
284 **Air de Lia** (*L'Enfant prodigue*)
French Arias and Songs. Bidú Sayao. Ody Y33130
285 **Aquarelles** (Green; Spleen). *See also* **286**
Debussy and Ravel. Yolanda Marcoulescou. Orion ORS 78312
286 **Ariettes oubliées** (C'est l'extase; Il pleure dans mon coeur; L'Ombre des
arbres; Chevaux de bois; Green; Spleen)
Fauré and Debussy. Elly Ameling. Col M-37210
Poems of Paul Verlaine. Carole Bogard. Cam CRS 2774
Debussy and Schoenberg. Charlotte Lehmann. EMI IC 065-46 356
287 **Beau soir**
Lieder and Chansons. Gérard Souzay. Sera S-60251
288 **Chansons de Bilitis** (La Flûte de Pan; La Chevelure; Le Tombeau des
naïades)
Fauré and Debussy. Elly Ameling. Col M-37210
Lieder Recital. Julia Hamari. Hung SLPX-12406
Song Recital. Frederica Von Stade. Col M-35127
289 **Chevaux de bois.** *See also* **286**
Debussy and Ravel. Yolanda Marcoulescou. Orion ORS 78312
290 **Colloque sentimental** (*Fêtes galantes II*). *See also* **294**
Debussy and Ravel. Yolanda Marcoulescou. Orion ORS 78312
291 **De fleur** (*Proses lyriques*). *See also* **302**
French Arias and Songs. Bidú Sayao. Ody Y33130
292 **Fantoches** (*Fêtes galantes I*). *See also* **293**
Debussy and Ravel. Yolanda Marcoulescou. Orion ORS 78312

DEBUSSY, Claude—*continued*
293 **Fêtes galantes I** (En sourdine; Fantoches; Clair de lune)
   Poems of Paul Verlaine. Carole Bogard. Cam CRS 2774
   Debussy and Schoenberg. Charlotte Lehmann. EMI IC 965-46 356
294 **Fêtes galantes II** (Les Ingénus; Le Faune; Colloque sentimental)
   Debussy and Schoenberg. Charlotte Lehmann. EMI IC 065-46 356
295 **Green.** See also **285** and **286**
   Lieder and Chansons. Gérard Souzay. Sera S-60251
296 **Jane**
   Mélodies françaises. Mady Mesplé. Odeon 2C 069-14089
297 **Le Jet d'eau**
   Debussy and Ravel. Yolanda Marcoulescou. Orion ORS 78312
298 **Je voudrais qu'il fut** (*La Damoiselle élue*)
   French Arias and Songs. Bidú Sayao. Ody Y33130
299 **Mandoline**
   Poems of Paul Verlaine. Carole Bogard. Cam CRS 2774
   Debussy and Ravel. Yolanda Marcoulescou. Orion ORS 78312
300 **Noël des enfants qui n'ont plus de maisons**
   A Recital of French Songs. Jill Gomez. Saga 5388
301 **Pour ce que plaisance est morte** (*Trois Chansons de France*). *See also* **306**
   Aufbruch des 20. Jahrhunderts im Lied. Dietrich Fischer-Dieskau.
   Odeon C 06502676
302 **Proses lyriques** (De rêve; De grève; De fleur; De soir)
   A Recital of French Songs. Jill Gomez. Saga 5388
303 **Quatres Chansons de Jeunesse** (Pantomime; Clair de lune; Pierrot;
   Apparition)
304 **Rondel chinois**
   Mélodies françaises. Mady Mesplé. Odeon 2C 069-14089
305 **Le Temps a laissié son manteau** (*Trois Chansons de France*). *See also* **306**
   Aufbruch des 20. Jahrhunderts im Lied. Odeon C 06502676
306 **Trois Chansons de France** (Le Temps a laissié son manteau; La Grotte;
   Pour ce que plaisance est morte)
   Debussy and Ravel. Yolanda Marcoulescou. Orion ORS 78312

DE LARA, Isadore (1858-1935)
307 **Rondel de l'adieu**
   An Album of French Songs. Martial Singher. 1750 Arch S-1766

DELIBES, Leo (1836-91)
308 **Les Filles de Cadix**
   Plaisir d'amour. Beverly Sills. Col M-33933
   Serate musicali. Joan Sutherland. Lon OSA-13132

DELIUS, Frederick (1862-1934)
309 The Birds' Story
310 Hidden Love
311 The Homeward Way
312 The Nightingale
    English Songs. Ian Partridge. Peters PLE 136/7
313 To Daffodils
    English Songs. Peter Pears. Argo ZK 28-29
314 Twilight Fancies
315 Young Venevil
    English Songs. Ian Partridge. Peters PLE 136/7

DELL'ACQUA, Eva (b. 1860)
316 Villanelle
    Plaisir d'amour. Beverly Sills. Col M-33933

DELLO JOIO, Norman (b. 1913)
317 The Listeners
    Anthology of American Music. William Parker. NW 300

DESSAU, Paul (b. 1894)
318 Noch bin ich eine Stadt
319 Such nicht mehr, Frau
    Wirkung der neuen Wiener Schule im Lied. Dietrich Fischer-Dieskau.
    Odeon C 06502677

DONIZETTI, Gaetano (1797-1848)
320 A mezzanotte
    Recital. Leyla Gencer. Cetra LPO 2003
    Serate musicali. Joan Sutherland. Lon OSA-13132
321 La corrispondenza amorosa
    Recital. Leyla Gencer. Cetra LPO 2003
    Songs. Renata Scotto. RCA AGLI 1-1341
322 J'attend toujours
    Serate musicali. Joan Sutherland. Lon OSA-13132
323 Una lagrima
    Songs. Renata Scotto. RCA AGLI 1-1341
324 La Mère et l'enfant
    Recital. Leyla Gencer. Cetra LPO 2003
    Songs. Renata Scotto. RCA AGLI 1-1341
325 Ne ornera la bruna chioma
    Songs. Renata Scotto. RCA AGLI 1-1341
326 Il sospiro
    Serate musicali. Joan Sutherland. Lon OSA-13132

DOWLAND, John (1562-1626)
327 **Awake, Sweet Love**
An English Song Recital. Peter Pears. Eclipse ECS 545
328 **Come Again, Sweet Love**
Song Recital. Frederica Von Stade. Col M-35127
329 **In Darkness Let Me Dwell**
An English Song Recital. Peter Pears. Eclipse ECS 545
330 **Sorrow, Stay**
Song Recital. Frederica Von Stade. Col M-35127

DUKE, John (b. 1899)
331 **Five Songs on Texts by Sara Teasdale** (All Beauty Calls You to Me;
Listen, I Love You; I Am So Weak a Thing; All Things in All the World;
O, My Love)
332 **Four Chinese Love Lyrics** (Waiting; Tucked up Skirts; Incense and
Moonlight; The Fifth Watch of the Night)
333 **Four Poems by e. e. cummings** (Just-Spring; i carry your heart; hist,
whist; The mountains are dancing)
334 **Four Poems by Emily Dickinson** (New Feet within My Garden Go; The
Rose Did Caper on Her Cheek; Have You a Brook in Your Little Heart;
I Taste a Liquor Never Brewed)
Songs by John Duke. Carole Bogard. Cam CRS 2776
335 **Luke Havergal**
336 **Miniver Cheevy**
337 **Richard Cory**
But Yesterday Is Not Today. Donald Gramm. NW 243
338 **Six Poems by Emily Dickinson** (Good Morning-Midnight; Heart, We Will
Forget Him; Let Down the Bars, Oh Death; An Awful Tempest Mashed
the Air; Nobody Knows This Little Rose; Bee, I'm Expecting You)
339 **Stopping by Woods on a Snowy Evening**
Songs by John Duke. Carole Bogard. Cam CRS 2776

DUPARC, Henri (1848-1933)
340 **Au pays où se fait la guerre**
Chausson and Duparc. Janet Baker. Ang S-37401
Duparc. Jane Rhodes. EMI C 169-16387
Song Recital. Kiri Te Kanawa. Col M-36667
341 **Chanson triste**
Ein Liederabend. Elly Ameling. EMI 063-02375
French Songs. Jessye Norman. Phi 9500 356
Fauré and Duparc. Ian Partridge. Pearl SHE 524

Duparc. Jane Rhodes. EMI C 169-16387
French Arias and Songs. Bidú Sayao. Ody Y33130
An Album of French Songs. Martial Singher. 1750 Arch S-1766

342 Elégie
Duparc. Jane Rhodes. EMI C 169-16387

343 Extase
Fauré and Duparc. Ian Partridge. Pearl SHE 524
Duparc. Jane Rhodes. EMI C 169-16387

344 Le Galop
Duparc. Jane Rhodes. EMI C 169-16387

345 L'Invitation au voyage
Chausson and Duparc. Janet Baker. Ang S-37401
French Songs. Jessye Norman. Phi 9500 356
Duparc. Jane Rhodes. EMI C 069-16387
Lieder and Chansons. Gérard Souzay. Sera S-60251
Song Recital. Kiri Te Kanawa. Col M-36667

346 Lamento
Duparc. Jane Rhodes. EMI C 169-16387

347 Le Manoir de Rosemonde
Chausson and Duparc. Janet Baker. Ang S-37401
Duparc. Jane Rhodes. EMI C 169-16387
An Album of French Songs. Martial Singher. 1750 Arch S-1766
Song Recital. Kiri Te Kanawa. Col M-36667

348 Phidylé
Duparc and Chausson. Janet Baker. Ang S-37401
French Songs. Jessye Norman. Phi 9500 356
Fauré and Duparc. Ian Partridge. Pearl SHE 524
Duparc. Jane Rhodes. EMI C 069-16387
An Album of French Songs. Martial Singher. 1750 Arch S-1766
Lieder and Chansons. Gérard Souzay. Sera S-20651

349 Sérénade Florentine

350 Soupir
Duparc. Jane Rhodes. EMI C 169-16387

351 Testament
Fauré and Duparc. Ian Partridge. Pearl SHE 524
Duparc. Jane Rhodes. EMI C 169-16387

352 La Vague et la cloche
Duparc. Jane Rhodes. EMI C 169-16387

353 La Vie antérieure
Duparc and Chausson. Janet Baker. Ang S-37401
French Songs. Jessye Norman. Phi 9500 356
Duparc. Jane Rhodes. EMI C 169-16387
An Album of French Songs. Martial Singher. 1750 Arch S-1766

DUPONT, Gabriel (1878-1914)
354 Mandoline
Poems of Paul Verlaine. Carole Bogard. Cam CRS 2774

DURANTE, Francesco (1684-1755)
355 Danza, danza, fanciulla gentile
Arie amorose. Janet Baker. Phi 9500 557
Songs of the Italian Baroque. Carlo Berganzi. HNH 4008
Von Stade Live. Frederica Von Stade. Col IM-37231

DUREY, Louis (1889-1979)
356 La Boule de neige
357 La Grenade
358 La Métempsychose
Songs by Le Groupe des Six. Carole Bogard. Cam 2777
359 Songs from Le Bestiaire de Apollinaire (La Tortue; Le Cheval; La Chevre
du Thibet; Le Serpent; La Puce; La Sauterelle; La Poulpe; Le Boeuf)
Songs of Les Six. Maria Lagios. Spectrum SR-147

DVORAK, Antonin (1841-1904)
360 Als die alte Mutter
Think on Me. Elly Ameling. CBS 36682

EDWARDS, George (b. 1943)
361 Veined Variety (Spring and Fall; Heaven-Haven; Canon I; At the Wedding
March; Spelt from Sibyl's Leaves; Pied Beauty)
Polin, Zahler and Edwards. Johana Arnold. Opus One 62

EINEM, Gottfried von (b. 1918)
362 In der Fremde
363 Ein junger Dichter denkt an die Geliebte
Wirkung der neuen Wiener Schule im Lied. Dietrich Fischer-Dieskau.
Odeon C 06502677

EISLER, Hanns (1898-1962)
364 An die Hoffnung
365 In der Frühe
366 Spruch
Wirkung der neuen Wiener Schule im Lied. Dietrich Fischer-Dieskau.
Odeon C 06502677

ESTEVE, Pablo (d. 1794)
367 Alma, sintamos!
   Canciones españolas. Teresa Berganza. DG 2530 598

EULENBURG, Philipp zu (1847-1921)
368 Liebessehnsucht
   Lieder der Neudeutschen. Dietrich Fischer-Dieskau. Odeon C 06502674

EVETT, Robert (1922-75)
369 Billy in the Darbies
   An American Song Recital. William Parker. NW 305

FALLA, Manuel de (1876-1946)
370 Jota *(Siete canciones populares españolas). See also* 373
   De los Angeles in Concert. Victoria de los Angeles. Ang SZ-37546
371 Oracion de las Madres que tienen a sus hijos en brazos
   Song Recital. Montserrat Caballé. Lon OS 26617
372 Polo *(Siete canciones populares españolas). See also* 373
   De los Angeles in Concert. Victoria de los Angeles. Ang SZ-37546
373 Siete canciones populares españolas (El pano moruno; Seguidilla
   murciana; Asturiana; Jota; Nana; Canción; Polo). *See also* **370** and **372**
   Canciones populares españolas. Teresa Berganza. DG 2530 875
   Seven Popular Spanish Songs. Montserrat Caballé. Lon OS 26575
   A Recital of Spanish Songs. Jill Gomez. Saga 5409
374 Trois Mélodies (Les Colombes; Chinoiserie; Séguidille)
   A Recital of Spanish Songs. Jill Gomez. Saga 5409
375 Tus ojillos negros
   Song Recital. Montserrat Caballé. Lon OS 26617

FAURÉ, Gabriel (1845-1924)
376 Complete Songs
   Elly Ameling and Gérard Souzay. Connoisseur CS-2127/8
   Jacques Herbillon, Anne-Marie Rodde, Sonia Nigoghossian. MHS
   3438/3448
377 A Clymène. *See also* **391**
   Poems of Paul Verlaine. Carole Bogard. Cam CRS 2774
378 Aprés un rêve
   Ein Liederabend. Elly Ameling. EMI 063-02375
   Fauré and Duparc. Ian Partridge. Pearl SHE 524
   Song Recital. Kiri Te Kanawa. Col M-36667
379 Arpège
   Mélodies françaises. Mady Mesplé. Odeon 2C 069-14089

FAURÉ, Gabriel—*continued*

380 Aubade
   Fauré and Duparc. Ian Partridge. Pearl SHE 524
381 Aurore
   Mélodies françaises. Mady Mesplé. Odeon 2C 069-14089
   Fauré and Duparc. Ian Partridge. Pearl SHE 524
382 Barcarolle
   Fauré and Duparc. Ian Partridge. Pearl SHE 524
383 Les Berceaux
   Lieder and Chansons. Gérard Souzay. Sera S-20651
384 La Bonne Chanson (Une Sainte en son auréole; Puisque l'aube grandit; La Lune blanche dans les bois; J'allais par des chemins perfides; J'ai presque peur, en vérité; Avant que tu ne t'en ailles; Donc, ce sera par un clair jour d'été)
   Fauré and Debussy. Elly Ameling. Col M 37210
   Songs. Carole Bogard. Cam CRS-2775
   Fauré, Poulenc and Ravel. Dietrich Fischer-Dieskau. HNH 4045
385 Chanson d'amour
   Fauré and Duparc. Ian Partridge. Pearl SHE 524
386 La Chanson du pêcheur
   Lieder and Chansons. Gérard Souzay. Sera S-60251
387 Clair de lune
388 En prière
   Fauré and Duparc. Ian Partridge. Pearl SHE 524
389 Lydia
   Mélodies françaises. Mady Mesplé. Odeon 2C 069-14089
390 Mai
   Lieder and Chansons. Gérard Souzay. Sera S-60251
391 Mélodies, op. 58 (Mandoline; En sourdine; Green; A Clymène; C'est l'extase; Spleen)
   Poems of Paul Verlaine. Carole Bogard. Cam CRS-2774
392 Nell
   Fauré and Duparc. Ian Partridge. Pearl SHE 524
   Song Recital. Kiri Te Kanawa. Col M-36667
393 Notre amour
   Mélodies françaises. Mady Mesplé. Odeon 2C 069-14089
394 Le Papillon et la fleur
   Serate musicali. Joan Sutherland. Lon OSA-13132
395 Poème d'un jour (Recontre; Toujours; Adieu)
396 Le Secret
   Fauré and Duparc. Ian Partridge. Pearl SHE 524
397 Spleen. *See also* **391**
   Poems of Paul Verlaine. Carole Bogard. Cam CRS 774

FINE, Irving (1914-62)
398 Four Songs from "Childhood Fables for Grownups" (Two Worms; The Duck and the Yak; Lenny the Leopard; Tigeroo)
    Anthology of American Music. William Parker. NW 300

FORD, Thomas (1580-1648)
399 Fair, Sweet, Cruel
    An English Song Recital. Peter Pears. Eclipse ECS 545

FORTNER, Wolfgang (b. 1907)
400 Abbitte
401 Hyperions Schicksalslied
402 Lied vom Weidenbaum
    Aufbruch des 20. Jahrhunderts im Lied. Dietrich Fischer-Dieskau. Odeon C 06502676

FRANZ, Robert (1815-92)
403 Abends
404 Auf dem Meere (An die bretterne Schiffswand)
405 Auf dem Meere (Aus den Himmelsaugen drober)
406 Auf dem Meere (Das Meer hat seine Perlen)
    Lieder der Schumannianer. Dietrich Fischer-Dieskau. Odeon C 06502673
407 Aus meinen grossen Schmerzen
    German Romantic Songs. Elly Ameling. Phi 9500 350
408 Bitte
    Lieder der Schumannianer. Dietrich Fischer-Dieskau. Odeon C 06502673
409 Dies und Das
    Farewell Recital. Lotte Lehmann. Pel LP 2009
410 Für Musik
    Lieder der Schumannianer. Dietrich Fischer-Dieskau. Odeon C 06502673
    Farewell Recital. Lotte Lehmann. Pel LP 2009
411 Gewitternacht
    Lieder der Schumannianer. Dietrich Fischer-Dieskau. Odeon C 06502673
412 Gute Nacht
    Farewell Recital. Lotte Lehman. PEL LP 2009
413 Mailied
    Lieder der Schumannianer. Dietrich Fischer-Dieskau. Odeon C 06502673

FRANZ, Robert—*continued*
414 Ständchen
415 Weisst du noch
    Farewell Recital. Lotte Lehmann. Pel LP 2009
416 Wie des Mondes Abbild
417 Wonne der Wehmut
    Lieder der Schumannianer. Dietrich Fischer-Dieskau. Odeon
    C 06502673

FRICKER, Peter Racine (b. 1920)
418 O Mistress Mine
    Music for Voice and Guitar. Peter Pears. RCA AGLI-1281

GARCIA LORCA, Federico (1899-1936)
419 Trece canciones españolas antiguas (Anda, Jaleo; Los cuatro muleros;
    Las tres hojas; Los mazos de monleón; Las morillas de jaén; Sevillanas
    del siglo XVIII; El café de Chinitas; Nana de Sevilla; Los pelegrinitos;
    Zorongo; Romance de Don Boyso; Los reyes de la baraja; La tarara)
    Canciones populares españolas. Teresa Berganza. DG 2530 875

GERSHWIN, George (1898-1937)
420 By Strauss
    Think on Me. Elly Ameling. CBS 36682

GIBBS, Cecil Armstrong (1889-1960)
421 The Fields Are Full
422 A Song of Shadows
    An Album of English Songs. Ian Partridge. MHS 4531

GIDEON, Miriam (b. 1906)
  423 The Condemned Playground (Pyrrha; Hiroshima; The Litanies of Satan)
    American Contemporary Vocal Music. Phyllis Bryn-Julson,
      Constantine Cassolas. CRI SD 343
  424 Nocturnes (To the Moon; High Tide; Witchery)
    Gideon and Boykan. Judith Raskin. CRI SD 401
  425 Questions on Nature
    American Contemporary Vocal Music. Jan De Gaetani. CRI SD 343
  426 Songs of Youth and Madness (To the Fates; To Diotima; Der gut Glaube;
    The Walk)
    Gideon and Boykan. Judith Raskin. CRI SD 401

GIORDANI, Tommaso (1730-1806)
427 Caro mio ben
    Arie amorose. Janet Baker. Phi 9500 557
    Songs of the Italian Baroque. Carlo Berganzi. HNH 4008
    Arie antiche. Montserrat Caballé. Lon OS 26618

GLUCK, Christoph Willibald (1714-87)
428 O del mio dolce ardor (*Parido ed Elena*)
    Recital. Cathryn Ballinger. Orion ORS 77280
    Eighteenth Century Arias. Renata Tebaldi. Lon OS 26376

GODARD, Benjamin (1849-95)
429 Chanson de Florian
    Serate musicali. Joan Sutherland. Lon OSA-13132

GOTTLIEB, Jack (b. 1930)
430 Downtown Blues for Uptown Halls (Big Little Girl; Impulsive; Neon Night)
    The Ariel Ensemble. Julia Lovett. Orion 81411

GOUNOD, Charles (1818-93)
431 Aimons-nous
    Lieder and Chansons. Gérard Souzay. Sera S-20651
432 Au printemps
    Serate musicali. Joan Sutherland. Lon OSA-13132
433 Biondina bella
    Reynaldo Hahn and His Songs. Reynaldo Hahn. Roc 5365
434 Chanson de printemps
435 La Naïade
436 O ma belle rebelle
    Mélodies françaises. Mady Mesplé. Odeon 2C 069-14089
437 Où voulez-vous aller?
    Lieder and Chansons. Gérard Souzay. Sera S-60251
438 Sérénade
    Mélodies françaises. Mady Mesplé. Odeon 2C 069-14089
439 Venise
440 Viens! Les Gazons sont verts
    Songs. Carole Bogard. Cam CRS-2775
441 Waltz (*Mireille*)
    Plaisir d'amour. Beverly Sills. Col M-33933

GRAINGER, Percy (1882-1961)
442 Bold William Taylor
    English Songs. Peter Pears. Argo ZK 28-29

GRANADOS, Enrique (1867-1916)
443 Cancó d'amor
    Seven Popular Spanish Songs. Montserrat Caballé. Lon OS 26575
444 Coleccion de tonadillas (Amor y odio; El majo discreto; El majo timido;
    El mirar de la maja; El tra la la y el punteado; La maja dolorosa)
    A Recital of Spanish Songs. Jill Gomez. Saga 5409
445 Elegia eterna
446 La maja y el ruisenor
    Seven Popular Spanish Songs. Montserrat Caballé. Lon OS 26575
447 El majo discreto. *See also* **444**
    Think on Me. Elly Ameling. CBS 36682
    Canciones españolas. Teresa Berganza. DG 2530 598
448 La maja dolorosa. *See also* **444**
    Canciones españolas. Teresa Berganza. DG 2530 598
    Song Recital. Montserrat Caballé. Lon OS 26617
449 El majo timido. *See also* **444**
    Canciones españolas. Teresa Berganza. DG 2530 598
450 L'ocell profeta
    Seven Popular Spanish Songs. Montserrat Caballé. Lon OS 26575
451 El tr la la y el punteado. *See also* **444**
    Canciones españolas. Teresa Berganza. DG 2530 598

GRIEG, Edvard (1843-1907)
452 Abschied
    Lieder der Schumannianer. Dietrich Fischer-Dieskau. Odeon
      C 06502673
453 Den Aergjerrige
    Grieg Songs. Kirsten Flagstad. Lon R 23220
454 Dereinst, Gedanke mein
    Lieder der Schumannianer. Dietrich Fischer-Dieskau. Odeon
      C 06502673
455 En Drom
456 Eros
457 Det forste mode
458 Fra Monte Pincio
459 Der Gynger en Bad pa Bolge
    Grieg Songs. Kirsten Flagstad. Lon R 23220
460 Hör'ich das Liedchen klingen
    Lieder der Schumannianer. Dietrich Fischer-Dieskau. Odeon
      C 06502673
461 Hytten
    Grieg Songs. Kirsten Flagstad. Lon R 23220

462 Ich liebe dich
 Ein Liederabend. Elly Ameling. EMI 063-02375
463 Jägerlied
 Lieder der Schumannianer. Dietrich Fischer-Dieskau. Odeon
 C 06502673
464 Jeg elsker Dig
465 Jeg giver mit digt til varen
 Grieg Songs. Kirsten Flagstad. Lon R 23220
466 Lauf der Welt
 Lieder der Schumannianer. Dietrich Fischer-Dieskau. Odeon
 C 06502673
467 I Liden hojt deroppe
468 Liden Kirsten
469 Med en Primula veris
470 Med en Vandlijie
471 Millom Rosor
 Grieg Songs. Kirsten Flagstad. Lon R 23220
472 Morgentau
 Lieder der Schumannianer. Dietrich Fischer-Dieskau. Odeon
 C 06502673
473 Ein Schwann
 To My Friends. Elisabeth Schwarzkopf. Lon OS 26592
474 Wo sind sie hin?
 Lieder der Schumannianer. Dietrich Fischer-Dieskau. Odeon
 C 06502673

GRIFFES, Charles Tomlinson (1884-1920)
475 Das ist ein Brausen und Heulen
476 Des Müden Abendlied
 An American Song Recital. William Parker. NW 305
477 Evening Song
 Songs. Alexandra Hunt. Orion 77272
478 The First Snowfall
 An American Song Recital. William Parker. NW 305
479 In a Myrtle Shade
 Songs. Alexandra Hunt. Orion 77272
480 An Old Song Resung
 An American Song Recital. William Parker. NW 305
481 Thy Dark Eyes to Mine
482 Waikiki
 Songs. Alexandra Hunt. Orion 77272
483 Wo ich bin, mich rings umdunkelt
484 Zwei Könige
 An American Song Recital. William Parker. NW 305

GUASTAVINO, Carlos (b. 1912)
485 La rosa y el sauce
 Think on Me. Elly Ameling. CBS 36682

GURIDI, Jesus (1886-1961)
486 **Seis canciones castellanas** (excerpts) (Llámale con el panuelo; No quiero tus avellanas; Cómo quieres que adivine)
 Canciones españolas. Teresa Berganza. DG 2530 598

GURNEY, Ivor (1890-1937)
487 **All Night under the Moon**
488 **Bread and Cherries**
489 **Brown Is My Love**
490 **The Cloths of Heaven**
491 **Desire in Spring**
492 **Down by the Salley Gardens**
493 **An Epitaph**
494 **The Fields Are Full**
495 **The Folly of Being Comforted**
 English Songs. Ian Partridge. Peters PLE 136/7
496 **Nine of the Clock**
497 **Ploughman Singing**
 An Album of English Songs. Ian Partridge. MHS 4531
498 **Severn Meadows**
499 **The Singer**
500 **Snow**
 English Songs. Ian Partridge. Peters PLE 136/7
501 **Under the Greenwood Tree**
 An Album of English Songs. Ian Partridge. MHS 4531

HAHN, Reynaldo (1874-1947)
502 **La Dernière Valse**
 Souvenirs. Elly Ameling. Col M 35119
503 **L'Enamourée**
504 **Etudes latines-Phillis**
505 **L'Heure exquise**
 Reynaldo Hahn and His Songs. Arthur Endreze. Roc 5365
506 **Infidélité**
 Mélodies françaises. Mady Mesplé. Odeon 2C 069-14089
507 **Je me mets en votre mercy**
 Reynaldo Hahn and His Songs. Guy Ferrant. Roc 5365

508 **Néère**
Mélodies françaises. Mady Mesplé. Odeon 2C 069-14089
509 **Offrande**
Hahn and His Songs. Reynaldo Hahn. Roc 5365
510 **Paysage triste**
511 **Le plus beau présent**
Hahn and His Songs. Guy Ferrant. Roc 5365
512 **Le Rossignol des lilas**
Think on Me. Elly Ameling. CBS 36682
513 **Si mes vers avaient des ailes**
Ein Liederabend. Elly Ameling. EMI 063-02375
514 **Le Temps d'aimer**
Hahn and His Songs. Guy Ferrant. Roc 5365
515 **Trois Jours de vendanges**
516 **Tyndaris**
Mélodies françaises. Mady Mesplé. Odeon 2C 069-14089
517 **Venezia-Chè pecà**
Hahn and His Songs. Reynaldo Hahn. Roc 5365

HALL, Carol (b. 1936)
518 **Jenny Rebecca**
Song Recital. Frederica Von Stade. Col M 35127

HANDEL, George Frideric (1685-1759)
519 **Ah, mio cor** (*Alcina*)
Recital. Cathryn Ballinger. Orion ORS 77280
520 **Un'alma innamorata**
521 **Armida abbondonata**
Italian Solo Cantatas. Marjanne Kweksilber. Tele 642367 AW
522 **Care selve** (*Atalanta*)
Scarlatti and Handel. Judith Blegen. Col M 34518
Pavarotti in Concert. Luciano Pavarotti. Lon OS-26391
523 **Crudel tiranno Amor** (cantata)
Handel. Elly Ameling. Phi 6670 113
524 **Eternal Source of Light Divine** (*Ode for Queen Anne's Birthday*)
Scarlatti and Handel. Judith Blegen. Col M 34518
525 **Figlio d'alte speranze**
Italian Solo Cantatas. Marjanne Kweksilber. Tele 642367 AW
526 **Let the Bright Seraphim** (*Samson*)
527 **Lusinghe più care** (*Alessandro*)
Scarlatti and Handel. Judith Blegen. Col M 34518

HANDEL, George Frideric *—continued*
528 **Nel dolce dell'oblio**
   Italian Solo Cantatas. Marjanne Kweksilber. Tele 642367 AW
529 **Neun deutsche Arien** (Künft'ger Zeiten eitler Kummer; Das zitternde
   Gläntzen; Süsser Blumen; Süsse Stille; Singe, Seele, Gott zum Preise;
   Meine Seele hört; Die ihr aus dunkeln Grüften; In den angenehmen
   Büschen; Flammende Rose)
   Handel. Catarina Ligendza. DG 2536 360
530 **O Had I Jubal's Lyre** (*Joshua*)
   The Art of Elisabeth Schumann. Sera 60320
531 **Ombra mai fù** (*Xerxes*)
   Eighteenth Century Arias. Renata Tebaldi. Lon OS 26376
532 **Piangerò la sorte mia** (*Giulio Cesare*)
   Handel. Elly Ameling. Phi 6670 113
   Recital of Songs and Arias. Renata Tebaldi. Lon R 23219
533 **Silete venti** (motet)
   Handel. Elly Ameling. Phi 6670 113
534 **Vanne, sorella ingrata** (*Radamisto*)
   Victoria de los Angeles in Concert. Ang SZ-37546
535 **Verdi prati** (*Alcina*)
   Eighteenth Century Arias. Renata Tebaldi. Lon OS 26376

HAUER, Joseph Matthias (1883-1959)
536 **An die Parzen**
537 **Der gefesselte Strom**
   Wirkung der neuen Wiener Schule im Lied. Dietrich Fischer-Dieskau.
   Odeon C 06502677

HAYDN, Franz Joseph (1732-1809)
538 **Complete Songs**
   Joseph Haydn Lieder. Elly Ameling. Phi 6769 064
539 **The Birks of Abergeldie**
540 **The Brisk Young Lad**
541 **Cumbernauld House**
542 **Duncan Gray**
543 **Green Grow the Rushes**
544 **I'm O'er Young to Marry Yet**
545 **John Anderson**
546 **Love Will Find Out the Way**
   Scottish Folk Songs. Janet Baker. Ang S-37172
547 **Mermaid's Song.** *See also* **538**
   Ein Liederabend. Elly Ameling. EMI C 063-02375

548 My Ain Kind Dearie
549 My Boy Tammy
550 O Bonny Lass
551 O Can Ye Sew Cushions?
552 The Ploughman
553 Shepherds, I Have Lost My Love
554 Sleepy Bodie
555 Up in the Morning Early
556 The White Cockade
   Scottish Folk Songs. Janet Baker. Ang S-37172

HELPS, Robert (b. 1928)
557 The Running Sun
   But Yesterday Is Not Today. Bethany Beardslee. NW 243

HENSEL, Fanny Mendelssohn (1805-47)
558 Du bist die Ruh
   Lieder. Katherine Ciesinski. Leonarda LPI 107
559 Gondellied
   Recital. Grayson Hirst. Leonarda LPI 112
560 Im Herbste
   Lieder. John Ostendorf. Leonarda LPI 107
561 Mayenlied
562 Morgenständchen
   Recital. Grayson Hirst. Leonarda LPI 112
563 Nachtwanderer
564 Die Nonne
565 Der Rosenkranz
   Lieder. John Ostendorf. Leonarda LPI 107
566 Schwanenlied
   Recital. Grayson Hirst. Leonarda LPI 112
567 Vorwurf
   Lieder. John Ostendorf. Leonarda LPI 107
568 Wanderlied
569 Warum sind denn die Rosen so blass
   Recital. Grayson Hirst. Leonarda LPI 112

HILLER, Ferdinand (1811-85)
570 Gebet
   Lieder der Schumannianer. Dietrich Fischer-Dieskau. Odeon
   C 06502673

HINDEMITH, Paul (1895-1963)
571 Fragment
   Aufbruch des 20. Jahrhunderts im Lied. Dietrich Fischer-Dieskau.
   Odeon C 06502676

HODDINOTT, Alun (b. 1929)
572 Roman Dream
   Hoddinott and Tate. Margaret Price. Decca ZRG 691

HOIBY, Lee (b. 1926)
573 Night Songs (Night; Pierrot; Angélique; The Shroud)
   American Songs. Carolyn Heafner. CRI SD 462

HOLST, Gustav (1874-1934)
574 The Floral Bandit
   An Album of English Songs. Ian Partridge. MHS 4531
575 Four Songs for Voice and Violin, op. 35 (Jesu Sweet; My Soul Has
   Naught but Fire and Ice; I Sing of a Maiden that Matchless Is; My Leman
   Is So True)
   Music for Voice and Violin. Catherine Malfitano. MHS 1976
576 A Little Music
   An Album of English Songs. Ian Partridge. MHS 4531
577 Persephone
   An English Song Recital. Peter Pears. Eclipse ECS 545
578 The Thought
   An Album of English Songs. Ian Partridge. MHE 4531

HONEGGER, Arthur (1892-1955)
579 Les Cloches. *See also* 576
580 Clotilde. *See also* 582
581 La Delphinium
   Songs by Le Groupe des Six. Carole Bogard. Cam 2777
582 Six Poèmes de Apollinaire (A la Santé; Clotilde; Automne; Les
   Saltimbanques; L'Adieu; Les Cloches)
   Songs of Les Six. Maria Lagios. Spectrum SR-147

HOVHANESS, Alan (b. 1911)
583 Hercules
   Songs for Voice and Violin. Catherine Malfitano. MHS 1876

HOWELLS, Herbert (b. 1892)
584 Alas Alack
585 Come Sing and Dance
586 The Dunce
587 King David
   Songs of Howells and Orr. Bruce Ogston. Unicorn RHS 369
588 The Lady Caroline
589 Merry Margaret
   Songs of Howells and Orr. Philip Langridge. Unicorn RHS 369
590 Miss T
   Songs of Howells and Orr. Bruce Ogston. Unicorn RHS 369
591 On the Merry First of May
592 The Three Cherry Trees
   Songs of Howells and Orr. Philip Langridge. Unicorn RHS 369

HULLEBROECK, Emiel (b. 1878)
593 Afrikaans Wiegeliedjie
   Souvenirs. Elly Ameling. Col M 35119

HUNDLEY, Richard (b. 1931)
594 The Astronomers
595 Come Ready and See Me
   Von Stade Live. Frederica Von Stade. Col IM-37231

IRELAND, John (1879-1962)
596 Friendship in Misfortune
   English Songs. Peter Pears. Argo ZK 28-29
   Twentieth Century English Songs. Peter Pears. Argo ZRG 5418
597 I Have Twelve Oxen
   An English Song Recital. Peter Pears. Eclipse ECS 545
598 The Land of Lost Content (The Lent Lily; Ladslove; Goal and Wicket;
   The Vain Desire; The Encounter; Epilogue)
599 Love and Friendship
600 The One Hope
601 The Trellis
   English Songs. Peter Pears. Argo ZK 28-29
   Twentieth Century English Songs. Peter Pears. Argo ZRG 5418

IVES, Charles (1874-1954)
602 Abide with Me
   Ives Songs. Dietrich Fischer-Dieskau. DG 2530 696

IVES, Charles—*continued*
  603 Ann Street
  604 At the River
       Ives Songs. Jan De Gaetani. None H 71325
       Ives Songs. Dietrich Fischer-Dieskau. DG 2530 696
       Anthology of American Music. William Parker. NW 300
  605 Autumn
       Ives Songs. Dietrich Fischer-Dieskau. DG 2530 696
  606 The Cage
       Ives Songs. Jan De Gaetani. None H 71325
  607 The Camp Meeting
  608 Chanson de Florian
       Anthology of American Music. William Parker. NW 300
  609 The Children's Hour
       Ives Songs. Dietrich Fischer-Dieskau. DG 2530 696
  610 A Christmas Carol
       Ives Songs. Jan De Gaetani. None H 71325
       Ives Songs. Dietrich Fischer-Dieskau. DG 2530 696
  611 The Circus Band
       Ives Songs. Jan De Gaetani. None H 71325
  612 Disclosure
       Ives Songs. Dietrich Fischer-Dieskau. DG 2530 696
  613 Elegie
       Ives Songs. Dietrich Fischer-Dieskau. DG 2530 696
       Anthology of American Music. William Parker. NW 300
  614 A Farewell to Land
       Ives Songs. Jan De Gaetani. None H 71325
       Ives Songs. Dietrich Fischer-Dieskau. DG 2530 696
  615 Feldeinsamkeit
       Ives Songs. Dietrich Fischer-Dieskau. DG 2530 696
  616 From "Paracelsus"
       Ives Songs. Jan De Gaetani. None H 71325
  617 From "The Swimmers"
       Ives Songs. Dietrich Fischer-Dieskau. DG 2530 696
  618 His Exaltation
       Anthology of American Music. William Parker. NW 300
  619 The Housatonic at Stockbridge
       Ives Songs. Jan De Gaetani. None H 71325
  620 Ich grolle nicht
       Ives Songs. Dietrich Fischer-Dieskau. DG 2530 696
  621 The Indians
       Ives Songs. Jan De Gaetani. None H 71325
  622 In Flanders Fields
       Ives Songs. Dietrich Fischer-Dieskau. DG 2530 696

623 The Innate
624 In the Mornin'
625 Like a Sick Eagle
626 Majority
    Ives Songs. Jan De Gaetani. None H 71325
627 Memories
    Souvenirs. Elly Ameling. Col M 35119
    Ives Songs. Jan De Gaetani. None H 71325
628 Qu'il m'irait
629 Rosamunde
    Anthology of American Music. William Parker. NW 300
630 Serenity
    Ives Songs. Jan De Gaetani. None H 71325
631 Sunrise
    Anthology of American Music. William Parker. NW 300
632 The Things Our Fathers Loved
633 Thoreau
    Ives Songs. Jan De Gaetani. None H 71325
634 Tom Sails Away
635 Two Little Flowers
    Ives Songs. Dietrich Fischer-Dieskau. DG 2530 696
636 Watchman
    Anthology of American Music. William Parker. NW 300
637 Weil' auf mir
638 West London
639 Where the Eagle
640 The White Gulls
    Ives Songs. Dietrich Fischer-Dieskau. DG 2530 696

JENSEN, Adolph (1837-79)
641 Lehn deine Wang' an meine Wang'
    Lieder der Schumannianer. Dietrich Fischer-Dieskau. Odeon
    C 06502673

JOLLES, Jerome
642 Wordsworth Songs (The World Is Too Much with Us; I Wandered Lonely
    as a Cloud)
    The Jubal Trio. Lucy Shelton. Grenadilla GS-1015

KIRCHNER, Fürchtegott Theodor (1823-1903)
643 Frühlingslied (Ich lieb' eine Blume)
644 Frühlingslied (In dem Walde spriesst)

KIRCHNER, Fürchtegott Theodor—*continued*
645 Frühlingslied (Leise zieht durch mein Gemüt)
646 Sie weiss es nicht
  Lieder der Schumannianer. Dietrich Fischer-Dieskau. Odeon
  C 06502673

KLEIN, Bernhard (1793-1832)
647 Der Erlkönig
  German Romantic Songs. Karl Markus. MHS 1962

KODALY, Zoltan (1882-1967)
648 Mónár Anna
649 Nausikaa
  Lieder Recital. Julia Hamari. Hung SLPX-12406

KOECHLIN, Charles (1867-1950)
650 Si tu le veux
  French Arias and Songs. Bidú Sayao. Ody Y33130
  Plaisir d'amour. Beverly Sills. Col M-33933

KRENEK, Ernst (b. 1900)
651 Erinnerung
652 Die frühen Gräber
  Wirkung der neuen Wiener Schule im Lied. Dietrich Fischer-Dieskau.
  Odeon C 06502677

LALO, Edouard (1823-92)
653 L'Esclave
  Serate musicali. Joan Sutherland. Lon OSA-13132

LANG, Josephine (1815-80)
654 Frühzeitiger Frühling
655 O sehntest du dich so nach mir
  Lieder. Katherine Ciesinski. Leonarda LPI 107
656 Wie glänzt so hell dein Auge
  Lieder. John Ostendorf. Leonarda LPI 107
657 Wie, wenn die Sonn'aufgeht
  Lieder. Katherine Ciesinski. Leonarda LPI 107
658 Der Winter
  Lieder. John Ostendorf. Leonarda LPI 107

LEONCAVALLO, Ruggero (1857-1919)
659 Sérénade française
Serenata. Renata Scotto. Col M-34501
Serate musicali. Joan Sutherland. Lon OSA-13132
660 Sérénade napolitaine
Serenata. Renata Scotto. Col M-34501

LISZT, Franz (1811-86)
661 Anfangs wollt ich fast verzagen
Liszt Lieder. Dietrich Fischer-Dieskau. DG 2740 254
Chabrier and Liszt. Paul Sperry. Orion ORS-75174
662 Blume und Duft
663 Comment, disaient-ils
664 Der du von dem Himmel bist
665 Des Tages laute Stimmen schweigen
666 Drei Lieder aus Schillers "Wilhelm Tell" (Der Fischerknabe; Der Hirt; Der Alpenjäger)
Liszt Lieder. Dietrich Fischer-Dieskau. DG 2740 254
667 Die drei Zigeuner
Liszt Lieder. Dietrich Fischer-Dieskau. DG 2740 254
Chabrier and Liszt. Paul Sperry. Orion ORS-75174
Song Recital. Frederica Von Stade. Col M 35127
668 Du bist wie eine Blume
Liszt Lieder. Dietrich Fischer-Dieskau. DG 2740 254
669 Einst
Song Recital. Frederica Von Stade. Col M 35127
670 Enfant, si j'étais roi
671 Englein hold im Lockengold
Liszt Lieder. Dietrich Fischer-Dieskau. DG 2740 254
672 Es muss ein Wunderbares sein
Think on Me. Elly Ameling. CBS 36682
Liszt Lieder. Dietrich Fischer-Dieskau. DG 2740 254
673 Es rauschen die Winde
Lieder der Neudeutschen. Dietrich Fischer-Dieskau. Odeon
   C 06502674
Liszt Lieder. Dietrich Fischer-Dieskau. DG 2740 254
674 Ein Fichtenbaum steht einsam
675 Gastbelza
676 Gestorben war ich
677 Hohe Liebe
678 Ich möchte hingehn
Liszt Lieder. Dietrich Fischer-Dieskau. DG 2740 254

LISZT, Franz—*continued*

679 **Ihr Auge**
    Chabrier and Liszt. Paul Sperry. Orion ORS-75174
680 **Ihr Glocken von Marling**
681 **Im Rhein, im schönen Strome**
682 **In Liebeslust**
683 **J'ai perdu ma force et ma vie**
    Liszt Lieder. Dietrich Fischer-Dieskau. DG 2740 254
684 **Kling leise, mein Lied**
    Liszt Lieder. Dietrich Fischer-Dieskau. DG 2740 254
    Chabrier and Liszt. Paul Sperry. Orion ORS-75174
685 **Lasst mich ruhen**
    Liszt Lieder. Dietrich Fischer-Dieskau. DG 2740 254
686 **Die Loreley**
    Liszt Lieder. Dietrich Fischer-Dieskau. DG 2740 254
    Chabrier and Liszt. Paul Sperry. Orion ORS-75174
687 **Morgens steh' ich auf und frage**
    Liszt Lieder. Dietrich Fischer-Dieskau. DG 2740 254
688 **Oh! quand je dors**
    Liszt Lieder. Dietrich Fischer-Dieskau. DG 2740 254
    Plaisir d'amour. Beverly Sills. Col M-33933
    Song Recital. Frederica Von Stade. Col M-35127
689 **O Lieb, so lang du lieben kannst**
    Souvenirs. Elly Ameling. Col M-35119
    Liszt Lieder. Dietrich Fischer-Dieskau. DG 2740 254
690 **Schwebe, schwebe, blaues Auge**
691 **S'il est un charmant gazon**
    Liszt Lieder. Dietrich Fischer-Dieskau. DG 2740 254
692 **Ständchen**
    Lieder der Neudeutschen. Dietrich Fischer-Dieskau. Odeon
        06502674
693 **Die stille Wasserrose**
694 **La Tombe et la rose**
695 **Der traurige Mönch**
696 **Tre sonetti di Petrarca** (Pace non trovo; Benedetto sia 'l giorno; I vidi in terra angelici costumi)
    Liszt Lieder. Dietrich Fischer-Dieskau. DG 2740 254
697 **Über allen Gipfeln ist Ruh'**
    Lieder der Neudeutschen. Dietrich Fischer-Dieskau. Odeon
        C 96592674
    Chabrier and Liszt. Paul Sperry. Orion ORS-75174
698 **Die Vätergruft**
    Liszt Lieder. Dietrich Fischer-Dieskau. DG 2740 254

699 Vergiftet sind meine Lieder
Liszt Lieder. Dietrich Fischer-Dieskau. DG 2740 254
Chabrier and Liszt. Paul Sperry. Orion ORS-75174
700 Le Vieux Vagabond
701 Wer nie sein Brot mit Tränen ass
Liszt Lieder. Dietrich Fischer-Dieskau. DG 2740 254
702 Wieder möcht'ich dir begegnen
Lieder der Neudeutschen. Dietrich Fischer-Dieskau. Odeon
C 06502674
Liszt Lieder. Dietrich Fischer-Dieskau. DG 2740 254
Chabrier and Liszt. Paul Sperry. Orion ORS-75174
703 Wie singt die Lerche schön
Liszt Lieder. Dietrich Fischer-Dieskau. DG 2740 254

LOEWE, Karl (1796-1867)
704 Der Fischer, op. 43/1
German Romantic Songs. Elly Ameling. Phi 9500 350
705 Graf Eberstein, op. 9/5
Ballads. Werner Hollweg. Tele 642620
706 Gregor auf dem Stein, op. 38 (Herolde ritten von Ort zu Ort; Im Schloss,
da brennen der Kerzen viel; Der junge König und sein Gemahl; Ein
Klippeneiland liegt im Meer; Wie bräutlich glänzt das heilige Rom)
Loewe. Roland Hermann. Claves D 8106
707 Harald, op. 45/1
Ballads. Werner Hollweg. Tele 642620
708 Kaiser Karl V (*Vier historische Balladen*), **op. 99** (Das Wiegenfest zu
Gent; Kaiser Karl V. in Wittenberg; Der Pilgrim vor St. Just; Die Leiche
zu St. Just)
Loewe. Roland Hermann. Claves D8106
709 Niemand hat's gesehn, op. 9/7
Ein Liederabend. Elly Ameling. EMI 063-02376
710 Die wandelnde Glocke, op. 20/3
To My Friends. Elisabeth Schwarzkopf. Lon OS 26592

LOTTI, Antonio (1667-1740)
711 Pur dicesti, o bocca bella
Arie amorose. Janet Baker. Phi 9500 557
Arie antiche. Montserrat Caballé. Lon OS 26618

LULLY, Jean-Baptiste (1632-87)
712 Bois épais (*Amadis*)
Hahn and His Songs. Reynaldo Hahn. Roc 5365

LUTYENS, Elisabeth (b. 1906)
713 **And Suddenly It's Evening** (On the Willow Boughs; In the Just Human
Time; Almost a Madrigal; And Suddenly It's Evening)
Lutyens and Bedford. Herbert Handt. Argo ZRG 638

MacDOWELL, Edward (1860-1908)
714 **Confidence**
715 **Folksong**
716 **Fra Nightingale**
717 **Midsummer Lullaby**
718 **The Swan**
719 **To a Wild Rose**
Songs. Alexandra Hunt. Orion 77272

MAHLER, Gustav (1860-1911)
720 **Ablösung in Sommer** (*Des Knaben Wunderhorn*)
German Romantic Songs. Elly Ameling. Phi 9500 350
721 **Lieder eines fahrenden Gesellen** (Wenn mein Schatz Hochzeit macht;
Ging heut'Morgen über's Feld; Ich hab'ein glühend Messer; Die zwei
blauen Augen)
Lieder. Dietrich Fischer-Dieskau. BWS IGI-382
722 **Wer hat dies Liedlein erdacht?** (*Des Knaben Wunderhorn*)
The Art of Elisabeth Schumann. Sera 60320
723 **Wo die schönen Trompeten blasen**
Aufbruch des 20. Jahrhunderts im Lied. Dietrich Fischer-Dieskau.
Odeon C 06502676

MAMLOK, Ursula (b. 1928)
724 **Haiku Settings**
The Jubal Trio. Lucy Shelton. Grenadella GS-1015

MARCELLO, Benedetto (1686-1739)
725 **Il mio bel foco**
Von Stade Live. Frederica Von Stade. Col IM-37231
726 **Quella fiamma che m'accende**
Arie antiche. Montserrat Caballé. Lon OS 26618

MARCHESI, Salvatore (1822-1908)
727 **La folletta**
Ein Liederabend. Elly Ameling. EMI 063-02375

MAROS, Miklós (b. 1943)
728 Descort
   Dorothy Dorow and Friends. Caprice RIKS LP 59

MARTIN, Frank (1890-1974)
729 Quatre Sonnets à Cassandre (Qui voudra voir comme un Dieu; Nature ornant la dame; Avant le temps; Quand je te vois)
   Mélodies. Carol Kimball. Orion ORS 82422
730 Unter der Linden
   Souvenirs. Elly Ameling. Col M 35119

MARTINI, Giovanni (1741-1816)
731 Plaisir d'amour
   Arie amorose. Janet Baker. Phi 9500 557
   Plaisir d'amour. Beverly Sills. Col M-33933
   Eighteenth Century Arias. Renata Tebaldi. Lon OS 26376

MARTUCCI, Giuseppe (1856-1909)
732 Al folto bosco
733 Cantava il ruscello
734 Sur mar al navicella
   Recital of Songs and Arias. Renata Tebaldi. Lon R 23219

MASCAGNI, Pietro (1863-1945)
735 M'ama non m'ama
736 La luna
737 Serenata
   Serenata. Renata Scotto. Col M-34501
738 La tua stella
   Serate musicali. Joan Sutherland. Lon OSA-13132

MASSENET, Jules (1842-1912)
739 Oh, si les fleurs avaient des yeux
740 Pensée d'automne
741 Puisqu'elle à pris ma vie
   Serate musicali. Joan Sutherland. Lon OSA-13132

MASETTI, Enzo (1893-1961)
742 Passo e non ti vedo
   Recital of Songs and Arias. Renata Tebaldi. Lon R 23219

MATTIESEN, Emil (1875-1939)
743 Heimgang in der Frühe
744 Herbstgefühl
    Lieder der Jahrhundertwende. Dietrich Fischer-Dieskau. Odeon
    C 06502675

MENDELSSOHN, Fanny. *See* HENSEL, Fanny Mendelssohn

MENDELSSOHN, Felix (1809-47)
745 Allnächtlich im Traume, op. 86/4
    Mendelssohn Lieder. Dietrich Fischer-Dieskau. EMI SLS 805
    German Romantic Songs. Karl Markus. MHS 1962
746 Altdeutsches Frühlingslied, op. 86/6
    German Romantic Songs. Karl Markus. MHS 1962
    On Wings of Songs. Peter Schreier. DG 2530 596
747 Altdeutsches Lied, op. 57/1
748 Altes Kirchenlied, op. 8/4
749 An die Entferne, op. 71/3
    Mendelssohn Lieder. Dietrich Fischer-Dieskau. EMI SLS 805
750 And'res Maienlied (*Hexenlied*), op. 8/8
    Mendelssohn Lieder. Dietrich Fischer-Dieskau. EMI SLS 805
    On Wings of Songs. Peter Schreier. DG 2530 596
751 Auf der Wanderschaft, op. 71/5
    Mendelssohn Lieder. Dietrich Fischer-Dieskau. EMI SLS 805
752 Auf Flügeln des Gesanges, op. 34/2
    Ein Liederabend. Elly Ameling. EMI 063 02375
    Mendelssohn Lieder. Dietrich Fischer-Dieskau. EMI SLS 805
    German Romantic Songs. Karl Markus. MHS 1962
    On Wings of Song. Peter Schreier. DG 2530 596
    The Art of Elisabeth Schumann. Sera 60320
753 Bei der Wiege, op. 47/6
    Mendelssohn Lieder. Dietrich Fischer-Dieskau. EMI SLS 805
    German Romantic Songs. Karl Markus. MHS 1962
    On Wings of Song. Peter Schreier. DG 2530 596
754 Der Blumenkranz, op. posth.
755 Da lieg' ich unter den Bäumen, op. 84/1
    Mendelssohn Lieder. Dietrich Fischer-Dieskau. EMI SLS 805
756 Des Mädchens Klage
    German Romantic Songs. Karl Markus. MHS 1962
757 Das erste Veilchen, op. 19a/2

Mendelssohn Lieder. Dietrich Fischer-Dieskau. EMI SLS 805
German Romantic Songs. Karl Markus. MHS 1962
758 Erster Verlust, op. 99/1
Mendelssohn Lieder. Dietrich Fischer-Dieskau. EMI SLS 805
On Wings of Song. Peter Schreier. DG 2530 596
759 Es lauschte das Laub, op. 86/1
Mendelssohn Lieder. Dietrich Fischer-Dieskau. EMI SLS 805
760 Frage, op. 9/1
On Wings of Song. Peter Schreier. DG 2530 596
761 Frühlingslied, op. 19a/1
762 Frühlingslied, op. 34/3
763 Frühlingslied, op. 47/3
Mendelssohn Lieder. Dietrich Fischer-Dieskau. EMI SLS 805
On Wings of Song. Peter Schreier. DG 2530 596
764 Gruss, op. 19a/5
Mendelssohn Lieder. Dietrich Fischer-Dieskau. EMI SLS 805
German Romantic Songs. Karl Markus. MHS 1962
On Wings of Song. Peter Schreier. DG 2530 596
765 Hirtenlied, op. 57/2
Mendelssohn Lieder. Dietrich Fischer-Dieskau. EMI SLS 805
On Wings of Song. Peter Schreier. DH 2530 596
766 Im Herbst, op. 9/5
On Wings of Song. Peter Schreier. DG 2530 596
767 Jägdlied, op. 84/3 (Des Knaben Wunderhorn)
Mendelssohn Lieder. Dietrich Fischer-Dieskau. EMI SLS 805
German Romantic Songs. Karl Markus. MHS 1962
On Wings of Song. Peter Schreier. DG 2530 596
768 Die Liebende schreibt, op. 86/3
German Romantic Songs. Elly Ameling. Phi 9500 350
769 Minnelied, op. 34/1 (Des Knaben Wunderhorn)
Mendelssohn Lieder. Dietrich Fischer-Dieskau. EMI SLS 805
On Wings of Song. Peter Schreier. DG 2530 596
770 Minnelied, op. 47/1
Mendelssohn Lieder. Dietrich Fischer-Dieskau. EMI SLS 805
771 Der Mond, op. 86/5
Mendelssohn Lieder. Dietrich Fischer-Dieskau. EMI SLS 805
Farewell Recital. Lotte Lehmann. Pel LP 2009
German Romantic Songs. Karl Markus. MHS 1962
On Wings of Song. Peter Schreier. DG 2530 596
772 Morgengruss, op. 47/2
773 Nachtlied, op. 71/6
Mendelssohn Lieder. Dietrich Fischer-Dieskau. EMI SLS 805
German Romantic Songs. Karl Markus. MHS 1962

MENDELSSOHN, Felix—*continued*

774 Neue Liebe, op. 19a/4
Mendelssohn Lieder. Dietrich Fischer-Dieskau. EMI SLS 805
German Romantic Songs. Karl Markus. MHS 1962
On Wings of Song. Peter Schreier. DG 2530 596

775 O Jugend, o schöne Rosenzeit, op. 57/4
Mendelssohn Lieder. Dietrich Fischer-Dieskau. EMI SLS 805

776 Pagenlied, op. posth.
Mendelssohn Lieder. Dietrich Fischer-Dieskau. EMI SLS 805
On Wings of Song. Peter Schreier. DG 2530 596

777 Reiselied, op. 19a/6
Mendelssohn Lieder. Dietrich Fischer-Dieskau. EMI SLS 805

778 Reiselied, op. 34/6
Mendelssohn Lieder. Dietrich Fischer-Dieskau. EMI SLS 805
German Romantic Songs. Karl Markus. MHS 1962
On Wings of Song. Peter Schreier. DG 2530 596

779 Scheidend, op. 9/6
Mendelssohn Lieder. Dietrich Fischer-Dieskau. EMI SLS 805

780 Schilflied, op. 71/4
Mendelssohn Lieder. Dietrich Fischer-Dieskau. EMI SLS 805
German Romantic Songs. Karl Markus. MHS 1962
On Wings of Song. Peter Schreier. DG 2530 596

781 Schlafloser Augen Leuchte, op. posth.
782 Tröstung, op. 71/1
Mendelssohn Lieder. Dietrich Fischer-Dieskau. EMI SLS 805

783 Venetianisches Gondellied, op. 57/5
Mendelssohn Lieder. Dietrich Fischer-Dieskau. EMI SLS 805
Farewell Recital. Lotte Lehmann. Pel LP 2009
German Romantic Songs. Karl Markus. MHS 1962
On Wings of Song. Peter Schreier. DG 2530 596

784 Volkslied, op. 47/4
785 Das Waldschloss, op. posth.
Mendelssohn Lieder. Dietrich Fischer-Dieskau. EMI SLS 805

786 Wanderlied, op. 57/6
Mendelssohn Lieder. Dietrich Fischer-Dieskau. EMI SLS 805
On Wings of Song. Peter Schreier. DG 2530 596

787 Warnung vor dem Rhein, op. posth.
788 Wenn sich zwei Herzen scheiden, op. 99/5
Mendelssohn Lieder. Dietrich Fischer-Dieskau. EMI SLS 805

789 Winterlied, op. 19a/3
Mendelssohn Lieder. Dietrich Fischer-Dieskau. EMI SLS 805
On Wings of Song. Peter Schreier. DG 2530 596

MEYERBEER, Giacomo (1791-1864)
790 Cantique du Trappiste
791 Le Chant du dimanche
792 Der Garten des Herzens
    Meyerbeer Lieder. Dietrich Fischer-Dieskau. DG 2533 295
793 Gegen mich selber in Hass entbrannt. *See* 797
794 Guide au bord ta nacelle
    Serate musicali. Joan Sutherland. Lon OSA-13132
795 Hör ich das Liedchen klingen
796 Komm
797 Menschenfeindlich
798 Mina
799 Le Poète mourant
800 Die Rose, die Lilie, die Taube
801 Die Rosenblätter
802 Scirocco
803 Sicilienne
804 Sie und ich
805 Ständchen
    Meyerbeer Lieder. Dietrich Fischer-Dieskau. DG 2533 295

MILHAUD, Darius (1892-1974)
806 L'Aurore
    Songs by Le Groupe des Six. Carole Bogard. Cam 2777
807 Chansons de poèmes juifs (Chant de nourrice; Chant de Sion; Chant
    d'amour; Chant de forgeron)
    Songs of Les Six. Maria Lagios. Spectrum SR-147
808 Fête de Bordeaux
809 Fête de Montmartre
810 Fumée
    Songs by Le Groupe des Six. Carole Bogard. Cam 2777
811 Lamentation
    Aufbruch des 20. Jahrhunderts im Lied. Dietrich Fischer-Dieskau.
    Odeon C 06502676
812 Six Chansons de théatre (La Bohémienne; Un Petit Pas; Mes amis les
    cygnes; Blancs sont les hours d'été; Je suis le filet; Chacun son tour)
    Mélodies. Carol Kimball. Orion ORS 82422

MOERAN, E. J. (1894-1950)
813 In Youth Is Pleasure
    An English Song Recital. Peter Pears. Eclipse ECS 545
814 The Merry Month of May
    English Songs. Peter Pears. Argo ZK 28-29

MONTEVERDI, Claudio (1567-1643)
815 Ahi troppo duro
  Portrayals of Love in Italian Song. Anna Gabrieli. Orion ORS-78307
816 Maledetto sia l'aspetto
817 Ohimè! Ch'io cado ohimè!
  Victoria de los Angeles in Concert. Ang SZ-37546
818 Quel sguardo sdegnosetto
  Portrayals of Love in Italian Song. Anna Gabrieli. Orion ORS-78307

MONTSALVATGE, Bassols Xavier (b. 1911)
819 Canción de cuna para dormir a un negrito. *See also* 820
  Think on Me. Elly Ameling. CBS 36682
820 Cinco canciones negras (Cuba dentro de un piano; Chévere; Punto de
  Habanera; Canción de cuna para dormir a un negrito; Canto negro)
  Canciones españolas. Teresa Berganza. DG 2530 598
  Song Recital. Montserrat Caballé. Ang SZB-3903
821 Punto de Habanera. *See also* 820
  Victoria de los Angeles in Concert. Ang SZ-37546

MORENO, Salvador (b. 1916)
822 Four Aztec Songs (No nantzin; Ihcuac tlaneci; To ilhuicac tlahtzin; To
  huey tlahtzin)
  Recital. Victoria de los Angeles. Col M 35139

MORET, Ernest
823 Le Nélumbo
  French Arias and Songs. Bidú Sayao. Ody Y33130

MORLEY, Thomas (1557-1602)
824 Come Sorrow, Come
825 Mistress Mine, Well May You Fare
  An English Song Recital. Peter Pears. Eclipse ECS 545

MOZART, Wolfgang Amadeus (1756-1791)
826 Lieder (complete)
  Mozart Lieder. Elly Ameling. Phi 6747 483
827 Abendempfindung, K. 523
  Mozart Lieder. Peter Schreier. Van VSD-71246
828 Ah, lo previdi . . . Ah, t'invola, K. 272
  Concert Arias. Kiri Te Kanawa. Lon OS 26661

829 **Ah, non lasciarmi, no,** K. 295a
    Concert Arias. Edita Gruberova. Lon OS 26662
830 **Alleluia** (*Exsultate jubilate*), K. 165
    The Art of Elisabeth Schumann. Sera 60320
831 **Alma grande e nobil core,** K. 578
    Concert Arias. Edita Gruberova. Lon OS 26662
832 **Als Luise die Briefe,** K. 520
    German Song. Benita Valente. Desmar DSM 1010
833 **L'amero, sara costante** (*Il re pastore*)
    The Art of Elisabeth Schumann. Sera 60320
834 **An Chloe,** K. 524
835 **Die betrogne Welt,** K. 474
    Mozart Lieder. Peter Schreier. Van VSD-71246
836 **Chi sa, chi sa, qual sia,** K. 582
    Concert Arias. Kiri Te Kanawa. Lon OS 26661
837 **Des kleinen Friedrichs Geburtstag,** K. 529
838 **Der Frühling,** K. 587
839 **Ich würd' auf meinem Pfad,** K. 390
840 **Das Kinderspiel,** K. 598
841 **Komm, liebe Zither, komm,** K. 351
842 **Lied der Freiheit,** K. 506
843 **Das Lied der Trennung,** K. 519
    Mozart Lieder. Peter Schreier. Van VSD-71246
844 **Misera, dove son . . . Ah, non son io che parlo,** K. 369
    Concert Arias. Edita Gruberova. Lon OS 26662
845 **Un moto do gioia,** K. 579
    Concert Arias. Edita Gruberova. Lon OS 26662
    German Songs. Benita Valente. Desmar DSM 1010
846 **Nehmt meinen Dank, ihr holden Gönner,** K. 383
847 **Non temer, amato bene,** K. 490
848 **Oh, temerario Arbace . . . Per quel paterno amplesso,** K. 79
    Concert Arias. Kiri Te Kanawa. Lon OS 26661
849 **Per pietà, bell'idol mio,** K. 78
    Concert Arias. Edita Gruberova. Lon OS 26662
850 **Resta, oh cara,** K. 528
    Concert Arias. Kiri Te Kanawa. Lon OS 26661
851 **Schon lacht der holde Frühling,** K. 580
    Concert Arias. Edita Gruberova. Lon OS 26662
852 **Sehnsucht nach dem Frühling,** K. 596
853 **Sei du mein Trost,** K. 391
    Mozart Lieder. Peter Schreier. Van VSD-71246
854 **Se tutti i mali miei,** K. 83
    Concert Arias. Edita Gruberova. Lon OS 26662

MOZART, Wolfgang Amadeus—*continued*
855 **Das Traumbild,** K. 530
　　Mozart Lieder. Peter Schrieier. Van VSD-71246
856 **Vado, ma dove?,** K. 583
　　Concert Arias. Kiri Te Kanawa. Lon OS 26661
857 **Das Veilchen,** K. 476
　　Mozart Lieder. Peter Schreier. Van VSD-71246
　　German Songs. Benita Valente. Desmar DSM 1010
858 **Voi avete un cor fidele,** K. 217
　　Concert Arias. Edita Gruberova. Lon OS 26662
859 **Wie unglücklich bin ich nit,** K. 147
　　Mozart Lieder. Peter Schreier. Van VSD-71246
860 **Der Zauberer,** K. 472
　　German Songs. Benita Valente. Desmar DSM 1010
861 **Die Zufriedenheit,** K. 369
　　Mozart Lieder. Peter Schreier. Van VSD-71246

MUSGRAVE, Thea (b. 1928)
862 **Primavera**
　　Dorothy Dorow and Friends. Caprice RIKS LP 59

MUSSORGSKY, Modest (1839-81)
863 **Darling Savishna**
864 **Eremushka's Lullaby**
865 **Hopak**
866 **The Orphan**
867 **Peasant's Lullaby**
868 **"Sunless" Cycle** (Between Four Walls; Thou Didst Not Know Me in the Crowd; The Idle, Noisy Day Is Ended; Ennui; Elegy; On the River)
869 **Where Art Thou Little Star?**
　　Russian Songs. Galina Vishnevskaya. EMI SLS 5055

NAKADA, Yoshinao (b. 1923)
870 **Oyasumi na sai**
　　Souvenirs. Elly Ameling. Col M 35119

NIETZSCHE, Friedrich (1844-1900)
871 **Nachspiel**
872 **Verwelkt**
873 **Wie Rebenranken schwingen**
　　Lieder der Neudeutschen. Dietrich Fischer-Dieskau. Odeon
　　C 06502674

NILES, John Jacob (1892-1980)
874 Evening
875 For My Brother, Reported Missing in Action, 1943
876 Love Winter when the Plant Says Nothing
   An American Song Recital. William Parker. NW 305

NIN, Joaquin (1879-1949)
877 Asturiana
   Victoria de los Angeles in Concert. Ang SZ-37546
878 Piano murciano
   Think on Me. Elly Ameling. CBS 36682
   Victoria de los Angeles in Concert. Ang SZ-37546

NORGARD, Per (b. 1932)
879 Wenn die Rose sich selbst schmückt
   Dorothy Dorow and Friends. Caprice RIKS LP 59

OBRADORS, Fernando J. (1897-1945)
880 Aquel sombrero de monte
881 Del cabello más sutil
882 El molondrón
883 El vito
   Song Recital. Montserrat Caballé. Lon OS 26617

OLDHAM, Arthur (b. 1926)
884 Three Chinese Lyrics (Herd Boy's Song; Fishing; Pedlar of Spells)
   An English Song Recital. Peter Pears. Eclipse ECS 545

ORGAD, Ben-Zion (b. 1926)
885 Shaar, Shaar
   The Cantilena Chamber Players. Elaine Bonazzi. Grenadilla
   GS-1029-30

ORR, C. W. (1893-1976)
886 Along the Field
887 Bahnhofstrasse
888 Farewell to Barn and Stack and Tree
889 In Valleys Green and Still
890 Is My Team Ploughing

ORR, C. W. —*continued*
891 The Lads in Their Hundreds
892 When I Watch the Living Meet
893 When Smoke Stood Up from Ludlow
894 While Summer On Is Stealing
895 With Rue My Heart Is Laden
　　　Songs of Howells and Orr. Philip Langridge, Bruce Ogston. Unicorn
　　　RHS 369

PAISIELLO, Giovanni (1740-1816)
896 Chi vuol la zingarella
897 La molinara
　　　Eighteenth Century Arias. Renata Tebaldi. Lon OS 26376
898 Nel cor più non mi sento
　　　Arie amorose. Janet Baker. Phi 9500 557
　　　Arie antiche. Montserrat Caballé. Lon OS 26618
　　　Eighteenth Century Arias. Renata Tebaldi. Lon OS 26376
899 I zingari in Fiera
　　　Eighteenth Century Arias. Renata Tebaldi. Lon OS 26376

PALADILHE, Emile (1844-1926)
900 Psyché
　　　Hahn and His Songs. Arthur Endreze. Roc 5465

PARRY, Hubert (1848-1918)
901 And Yet I Love Her till I Die
902 Blow, Blow Thou Winter Wind
903 Bright Star
904 From a City Window
905 Looking Backward
906 Love Is a Bable
907 O Mistress Mine
908 Marian
909 No Longer Mourn for Me
910 On a Time the Amorous Silvy
911 Take, O Take Those Lips Away
912 There
913 There Be None of Beauty's Daughters
914 Thine Eyes Still Shine for Me
915 Weep You No More
916 A Welsh Lullaby

917 **When Comes My Gwen**
918 **When Icicles Hang by the Wall**
919 **When Lovers Meet Again**
920 **When We Two Parted**
     Parry: English Lyrics. Robert Tear. Argo ZK 44

PERERA, Ronald (b. 1941)
921 **Three Poems of Günter Grass** (Gleisdreieck; Klappstühle; Schlaflos)
     Music and Words. Elsa Charlston. CRI S-420

PERGOLESI, Giovanni Battista (1710-36)
922 **Confusa, smarrita**
     Italian Baroque Songs. Teresa Berganza. DG 2531 192
923 **Ogni pena più spietata**
     Arie amorose. Janet Baker. Phi 9500 557
924 **Se tu m'ami**
     Italian Baroque Songs. Teresa Berganza. DG 2531 192
     Arie antiche. Montserrat Caballé. Lon OS 26618
925 **Stizzoso, mio stizzoso** (*La serva padrona*)
     Eighteenth Century Arias. Renata Tebaldi. Lon OS 26376
926 **Tre giorni son che Nina**
     Songs of the Italian Baroque. Carlo Berganzi. HNH 4008
     Eighteenth Century Arias. Renata Tebaldi. Lon OS 26376

PERLE, George (b. 1915)
927 **Thirteen Dickinson Songs** (From a Childhood: Perhaps You'd Like To
     Buy a Flower; I Like To See It Lap the Miles; I Know Some Lovely
     Houses off the Road; There Came a Wind Like a Bugle; Autumn Days:
     Beauty—Be Not Caused—It Is; The Wind-Tapped Like a Tired Man;
     These Are the Days When Birds Come Back; The Heart Asks Pleasure—
     First; Grave Hour: What If I Say I Shall Not Wait; If I'm Lost—Now;
     The Loneliness One Dare Not Sound; Under the Light, Yet Under;
     Closing Piece: She Bore It till the Simple Weins)
928 **Two Rilke Songs** (Du meine heilige Einsamkeit; Der Bach hat leise
     Melodien)
     Songs by George Perle. Bethany Beardslee. CRI SD 403

PEYTON, Malcomb (b. 1932)
929 **Songs from Walt Whitman** (Oh Me! Oh Life!; Roots and Leaves
     Themselves Alone Are These; Darest Thou Now O Soul; Scented
     Herbage of My Breast; Warble for Lilac-Time)
     O'Brien and Peyton. Bethany Beardslee. CRI SD 466

PFITZNER, Hans (1869-1949)
930 **An den Mond**
Lieder der Jahrhundertwende. Dietrich Fischer-Dieskau. Odeon
C 06502675
931 **Hussens Kerker**
Aufbruch des 20. Jahrhunderts im Lied. Dietrich Fischer-
Dieskau. Odeon C 06502676
932 **Ist der Himmel darum im Lenz so blau**
German Romantic Songs. Elly Ameling. Phi 9500 350
933 **Mailied**
Lieder der Jahrhundertwende. Dietrich Fischer-Dieskau. Odeon
C 06502675

PICCINNI, Niccolò (1728-1800)
934 **O notte o dea del mistero**
Arie amorose. Janet Baker. Phi 9500 557

PIZZETTI, Ildebrando (1880-1968)
935 **Donna Lombarda**
936 **Levommi il mio pensier**
Portrayals of Love in Italian Song. Anna Gabrieli. Orion ORS-78307
937 **I pastori**
Serenata. Renata Scotto. Col M-34501
938 **La pesca dell'anello**
939 **La prigioniera**
940 **Quel rossignol**
Portrayals of Love in Italian Song. Anna Gabrieli. Orion ORS-78307

PONCHIELLI, Amilcare (1834-86)
941 **Il trovatore**
Serate musicali. Joan Sutherland. Lon OSA-13132

POULENC, Francis (1899-1963)
942 **Air champêtre** (*Airs chantés*)
Songs by Le Groupe des Six. Carole Bogard. Cam 2777
943 **Air romantique** (*Airs chantés*)
944 **Air vif** (*Airs chantés*)
945 **A sa guitare** (*Cinq Poèmes de Ronsard*)
Songs of Les Six. Maria Lagios. Spectrum SR-147
946 **Attributs** (*Poèmes de Ronsard*)
Songs by Le Groupe des Six. Carole Bogard. Cam 2777

947 **Le Bal masqué** (Préambule et air de Bravoure; Intermède; Malvina;
    Bagatelle; La Dame aveugle; Caprice-Finale)
    Fauré, Poulenc and Ravel. Dietrich Fischer-Dieskau. HNH 4045
948 **Chanson Bretonne** (*Cinq Poèmes de Max Jacob*)
    Songs by Le Groupe des Six. Carole Bogard. Cam 2777
949 **Les Chemins de l'amour**
    Think on Me. Elly Ameling. CBS 36682
    French Songs. Jessye Norman. Phi 9500 356
    Plaisir d'amour. Beverly Sills. Col M-33933
950 **Deux Mélodies** (La Souris; Nuage)
951 **La Fraîcheur et le feu** (Rayon des yeux; Le Matin les branches attisent;
    Tout disparut; Dans les ténèbres du jardin; Unis la fraîcheur et le feu;
    Homme au sourire tendre; La Grande Rivière qui va)
    Mélodies. Carol Kimball. Orion ORS 82422
952 **La Grenouillère**
    French Songs. Jessye Norman. Phi 9500 356
953 **Hier** (*Trois Poèmes de Louise Lalanne*)
    Songs by Le Groupe des Six. Carole Bogard. Cam 2777
954 **Il vole** (Fiancailles pour rire)
    Songs of Les Six. Maria Lagios. Spectrum SR-147
955 **Montparnasse**
    French Songs. Jessye Norman. Phi 9500 356
956 **La Petite Servante** (*Cinq Poèmes de Max Jacob*)
    Songs by Le Groupe des Six. Carole Bogard. Cam 2777
957 **Quatre Poèmes d'Apollinaire** (L'Anguille; Carte postale; Avant le cinéma
    1904)
    Mélodies. Carol Kimball. Orion ORS 82422
958 **Souric et mouric** (*Cinq Poèmes de Max Jacob*)
    Songs of Les Six. Maria Lagios. Spectrum SR-147
959 **Le Tombeau** (*Poèmes de Ronsard*)
    Songs by Le Groupe des Six. Carole Bogard. Cam 2777
960 **Voyage à Paris**
    French Songs. Jessye Norman. Phi 9500 356

PUCCINI, Giacomo (1858-1924)
961 **Menti all'avviso**
962 **Sole e amore**
    Serenata. Renata Scotto. Col M-34501

PURCELL, Henry (1658-95)
963 **Ah! How Sweet It Is To Love** (*Tyrannic Love*)
    Sweeter than Roses. Ian Partridge. Enigma K 53569
964 **The Blessed Virgin's Expostulation**
    Song Recital. Frederica Von Stade. Col M 35127

PURCELL, Henry *—continued*

965 **Bonvica's Song** (*Bonduca*)

966 **Crown the Altar**

967 **The Earth Trembled** (On Our Saviour's Passion)
Sweeter than Roses. Ian Partridge. Enigma K 53569

968 **An Evening Hymn**
Purcell Songs. Alfred Deller. HM-249
Sweeter than Roses. Ian Partridge. Enigma K 53569

969 **Fairest Isle** (*King Arthur*)

970 **From Rosy Bow'rs**
Purcell Songs. Alfred Deller. HM-249

971 **I Attempt from Love's Sickness to Fly** (*Indian Queen*)

972 **If Music Be the Food of Love**
Purcell Songs. Alfred Deller. HM-249
Sweeter than Roses. Ian Partridge. Enigma K 53569

973 **I'll Sail upon the Dog-Star** (*A Fool's Preferment*)

974 **I See She Flies Me Ev'rywhere** (*Aurang-Zebe*)

975 **Let the Night Perish** (Job's Curse)

976 **Lord, What Is Man, Lost Man** (A Divine Hymn)

977 **A Morning Hymn**
Sweeter than Roses. Ian Partridge. Enigma K 53569

978 **Music for a While**
Souvenirs. Elly Ameling. Col M 35119
Purcell Songs. Alfred Deller. HM-249
Sweeter than Roses. Ian Partridge. Enigma K 53569

979 **Not All My Torments**

980 **O Lead Me to Some Peaceful Gloom**

981 **The Plaint**

982 **Retired from Any Mortal's Sight**
Purcell Songs. Alfred Deller. HM-249

983 **A Roundelay** (*The Mock Marriage*)
Sweeter than Roses. Ian Partridge. Enigma K 53569

984 **Since from My Dear Astrea's Sight**
Purcell Songs. Alfred Deller. HM-249
Sweeter than Roses. Ian Partridge. Enigma K 53569

985 **Sweeter than Roses** (*Pausanias*)
Britten and Purcell. James Bowman. Decca SXL 6608
Purcell Songs. Alfred Deller. HM-249
Sweeter than Roses. Ian Partridge. Enigma K 53569

986 **Take Not a Woman's Anger III** (*The Rival Sisters*)
Sweeter than Roses. Ian Partridge. Enigma K 53569

987 **Thrice Happy Lovers**
Purcell Songs. Alfred Deller. HM-249

QUILTER, Roger (1877-1953)
988 Go, Lovely Rose
989 O Mistress Mine
An Album of English Songs. Ian Partridge. MHS 4531

RACHMANINOFF, Sergei (1873-1943)
990 **Songs,** volume I (in Russian)
Daisies, op. 38/3; Dissonance, op. 34/13; Dreams, op. 38/5; The
Harvest of Sorrow, op. 4/5; How Fair This Spot, op. 21/7; In My Garden
at Night, op. 38/1; The Morn of Life, op. 34/10; The Muse, op. 34/1;
Oh, Never Sing to Me Again, op. 4/4; The Pied Piper, op. 38/4; The
Poet, op. 34/9; The Quest, op. 38/6; The Storm, op. 34/3; To Her,
op. 38/2; Vocalise, op. 34/14; What Wealth of Rapture, op. 34/12
Elisabeth Söderström. Lon OS-26428
991 **Songs,** volume II (in Russian)
Arion, op. 34/5; Believe It Not, op. 14/7; Day to Night Comparing
Went the Wind Her Way, op. 34/4; A Dream, op. 8/5; Fate, op. 21/1;
For a Life of Pain I Have Given My Love, op. 8/4; In the Silent Night,
op. 4/3; I Wait for Thee, op. 14/1; The Little Island, op. 14/2; Midsummer
Nights, op. 14/5; Music, op. 34/8; The Raising of Lazarus, op. 34/6;
So Dread a Fate I'll Ne'er Believe, op. 34/7; So Many Hours, So Many
Fancies, op. 4/6; Spring Waters, op. 14/11; The World Would See Thee
Smile, op. 14/6
Elisabeth Söderström. Lon OS-26453
992 **Songs,** volume III (in Russian)
The Answer, op. 21/4; Before My Window, op. 26/10; Before the
Image, op. 21/10; By the Grave, op. 21/2; The Fountains, op. 26/11;
Lilacs, op. 21/5; Loneliness, op. 21/6; Melody, op. 21/9; Night Is
Mournful, op. 21/12; No Prophet, op. 21/11; On the Death of a
Linnet, op. 21/8; Powder'd Paint; The Ring, op. 26/14; Sorrow in the
Springtime, op. 21/3; To the Children, op. 26/7; Twilight, op. 21/3
Elisabeth Söderström. Lon OS-26433
993 **Songs,** volume IV (in Russian)
Again You Leapt, My Heart; All Once I Gladly Owned, op. 26/2;
April! Vernal, Festive Time; Beloved, Let Us Fly, op. 26/5; Brooding,
op. 8/3; Come, Let Us Rest, op. 26/3; Daisies, op. 38/3; Christ Is Risen,
op. 26/6; The Heart's Secret, op. 26/1; How Few the Joys, op. 14/3;
I Came to Her, op. 14/4; I Shall Tell You Nothing; Like Blossom New-
Freshen'd to Gladness, op. 8/2; Morning, op. 4/2; Oh Stay, My Love,
Forsake Me Not, op. 4/1; A Prayer, op. 8/6; Twilight Has Fallen;
Two Partings, op. 26/4; The Water Lily, op. 8/1
Elisabeth Söderström. Lon OS-26559

RACHMANINOFF, Sergei—*continued*
994 **Songs,** volume V (in Russian)
All Things Depart, op. 26/15; As Fair as Day in Blaze of Noon, op. 14/9;
By the Gates of the Holy Dwelling; Do You Remember the Evening?;
A Flower Fell; From St. John's Gospel; Let Me Rest Here Alone,
op. 26/9; Letter to S. Stanislavski from S. Rachmaninov; Love's Flame,
op. 14/10; Night; O, Do Not Grieve, op. 14/8; Song of Disappointment;
The Soul's Concealment, op. 34/2; The Pity I Implore, op. 26/8; 'Tis
Time, op. 14/12; Were You Hiccoughing, Natasha?; When Yesterday
We Met, op. 26/13; With Holy Banner Firmly Held, op. 34/11
Elisabeth Söderström. Lon OS-26615
995 **All Love You So,** op. 14/6. *See also* **991**
Rachmaninoff Songs. Peter Del Grande. Orion ORS-75180
996 **The Answer,** op. 21/4. *See also* **992**
Songs. Jan De Gaetani. None H-71373
997 **A-oo (Was It a Dream),** op. 38/6. *See also* **990**
998 **At Night in My Garden,** op. 38/1. *See also* **990**
999 **Child! Like a Flower,** op. 8/2. *See also* **993**
Rachmaninoff Songs. Peter Del Grande. Orion ORS-75180
1000 **Christ Is Risen,** op. 26/6. *See also* **993**
Songs. Jan De Gaetani. None H-71373
1001 **Daisies,** op. 38/3. *See also* **990**
1002 **Dream,** op. 8/5. *See also* **991**
1003 **Dream,** op. 38/5. *See also* **990**
1004 **Floods of Spring,** op. 14/11. *See also* **991**
Rachmaninoff Songs. Peter Del Grande. Orion ORS-75180
1005 **The Harvest of Sorrow,** op. 4/5. *See also* **990**
Songs. Jan De Gaetani. None H-71373
1006 **He Took It All Away from Me,** op. 26/2. *See also* **993**
Rachmaninoff Songs. Peter Del Grande. Orion ORS-75180
1007 **How Long since Love,** op. 14/3. *See also* **993**
1008 **Lilacs,** op. 21/5. *See also* **992**
Songs. Jan De Getani. None H-71373
1009 **Love Has Lost Its Joy,** op. 14/3. *See also* **993**
1010 **Night Is Sad,** op. 21/12. *See also* **992**
Rachmaninoff Songs. Peter Del Grande. Orion ORS-75180
1011 **Oh, Do Not Grieve,** op. 14/8. *See also* **994**
1012 **A Passing Breeze,** op. 34/4. *See also* **991**
Songs. Jan De Gaetani. None H-71373
1013 **The Rat Catcher,** op. 38/4. *See also* **990**
Rachmaninoff Songs. Peter Del Grande. Orion ORS-75180
1014 **Spring Waters,** op. 14/11. *See also* **991**
Souvenirs. Elly Ameling. Col M 35119

1015 **Time,** op. 14/12. *See also* **994**
1016 **To Her,** op. 38/2. *See also* **990**
    Rachmaninoff Songs. Peter Del Grande. Orion ORS-75180
1017 **To the Children,** op. 26/7. *See also* **992**
    Songs. Jan De Gaetani. None H-71373
    Rachmaninoff Songs. Peter Del Grande. Orion ORS-75180
1018 **Water Lily,** op. 8/2. *See also* **993**
    Rachmaninoff Songs. Peter Del Grande. Orion ORS-75180

RAFF, Joseph Joachim (1822-82)
1019 **Unter den Palmen**
    Lieder der Neudeutschen. Dietrich Fischer-Dieskau. Odeon
    C 06502674

RAINER, Priaulx (b. 1903)
1020 **Cycle for Declamation** (Wee Cannot Bid the Fruits; In the Wombe of the
    Earth; Nunc, lento sonitu)
    English Songs. Peter Pears. Argo ZK 28-29
    Twentieth Century English Songs. Peter Pears. Argo ZRG 5418

RAVEL, Maurice (1875-1937)
1021 **Chanson de Rouet**
    Debussy and Ravel. Yolanda Marcoulescou. Orion ORS 78312
1022 **Chansons madécasses** (Nahandove; Aoua!; Il est doux)
    Fauré, Poulenc and Ravel. Dietrich Fischer-Dieskau. HNH 4045
1023 **Chants populaires** (Chanson espagnole; Chanson française; Chanson
    italienne; Chanson hébraïque)
    An Album of French Songs. Martial Singher. 1750 Arch S-1766
1024 **Cinq Mélodies populaires grecques** (Le Réveil de la mariée; Là-bas, ver
    l'église; Quel galant m'est comparable; Chanson des cueilleuses de
    lentisques; Tout gai)
    Von Stade Live. Frederica Von Stade. Col IM-37231
1025 **Deux Mélodies hébraïque** (L'Énigme éternelle; Kaddisch)
    French Songs. Jessye Norman. Phi 9500 356
1026 **Epigramme de Cl. Marot** (D'Anne qui me jecta de la neige; D'Anne
    jouant de l'espinette)
1027 **Les Grands Vents**
    Debussy and Ravel. Yolanda Marcoulescou. Orion ORS 78312
1028 **Histoires naturelles** (La Paon; Le Grillon; Le Cygne; Le Martin-Pêcheur;
    La Pintade)
    Ravel and Saite. Régine Crespin. Col 36666

RAVEL, Maurice—*continued*
1029 Manteau de fleurs
  Debussy and Ravel. Yolanda Marcoulescou. Orion ORS 78312
1030 Nicolette
  An Album of French Songs. Martial Singher. 1750 Arch S-1766
1031 Noël des jouets
1032 Rêves
1033 Ronsard à son âme
1034 Sainte
  Debussy and Ravel. Yolanda Marcoulescou. Orion ORS 78312
1035 Shéhérazade (Asie; La Flûte enchantée; L'Indifferent)
  Berlioz and Ravel. Jessye Norman. Phi 9500 783
1036 Sur l'herbe
  Debussy and Ravel. Yolanda Marcoulescou. Orion ORS 78312
1037 Toi, le coeur de la rose (*L'Enfant et les sortilèges*)
  French Arias and Songs. Bidú Sayao. Ody Y33130

REGER, Max (1873-1916)
1038 Maria Wiegenlied
  The Art of Elisabeth Schumann. Sera 60320
1039 Sommernacht
  Lieder der Jahrhundertwende. Dietrich Fischer-Dieskau. Odeon
  C 06502675
1040 Waldeinsamkeit
  German Romantic Songs. Elly Ameling. Phi 9500 350
1041 Warnung
  Lieder der Jahrhundertwende. Dietrich Fischer-Dieskau. Odeon
  C 06502675

REICHARDT, Louise (1779-1826)
1042 Bergmannslied
1043 Betteley der Vögel
1044 Die Blume der Blumen
1045 Duettino
1046 Heimweh
1047 Hier liegt ein Spielmann begraben
1048 Tre canzoni (Giusto amor; Notturno; Vanne felice rio)
  Recital. Grayson Hirst. Leonarda LPI 112

RESPIGHI, Ottorino (1879-1936)
1049 Au milieu du jardin
  Serenata. Renata Scotto. Col M-34501

1050 Nebbie
1051 Nevicata
1052 Pioggia
    Pavarotti in Concert. Luciano Pavarotti. Lon OS 26391
1053 Povero core
1054 Razzolan
1055 Soupir
    Serenata. Renata Scotto. Col M-34501
1056 I tempi assai lontani
    Serate musicali. Joan Sutherland. Lon OSA 13132
1057 Il tramonto
    Recital. Cathryn Ballinger. Orion ORA 77280

REUTTER, Hermann (b. 1900)
1058 Johann Kepler
1059 Lied für ein dunkles Mädchen
1060 Trommel
    Aufbruch des 20. Jahrhunderts im Lied. Dietrich Fischer-
    Dieskau. Odeon C 06502676

RITTER, Alexander (1833-96)
1061 Primula veris
    Lieder der Neudeutschen. Dietrich Fischer-Dieskau. Odeon
    C 06502674

ROCHBERG, George (b. 1918)
1062 Songs in Praise of Krishna
    Rochberg. Neva Pilgrim. CRI SD 360

RODRIGO, Joaquin (b. 1902)
1063 Canción del Grumete
    Victoria de los Angeles in Concert. Ang SZ-37546
1064 Cuatro madrigales amatorios (De dónde venis, amore?; Cón qué la
    lavaré; Vos me matásteis; De los álamos vengo, madre)
    Spanish Song Recital. Montserrat Caballé. Lon OS 26617
1065 De los álamos vengo, madre. *See also* 1064
    Souvenirs. Elly Ameling. Col M 35119
    Victoria de los Angeles in Concert. Ang SZ-37546
1066 Four Sephardic Songs (Respóndemos; Una postora yo ami; Nani, nani;
    "Morena" me llaman)
    Recital. Victoria de los Angeles. Col M 35129
1067 Trovadoresca
    Victoria de los Angeles in Concert. Ang SZ-37546

ROREM, Ned (b. 1923)
1068 **Ariel** (Words; Poppies in July; The Hanging Man; Poppies in October; Lady Lazarus)
Rorem. Phyllis Curtin. Desto DC 7147
1069 **Mourning Scene**
An American Song Recital. William Parker. NW 305

ROSSETER, Philip (1567-1623)
1070 **What Then Is Love but Mourning**
1071 **When Laura Smiles**
An English Song Recital. Peter Pears. Eclipse ECS 545

ROSSI, Luigi (1597-1653)
1072 **Erminia sventurata**
1073 **Gelosia**
1074 **Lamento della regina de svezia**
1075 **Lamento de Zaida Mora**
1076 **Mentre sorge dal mar**
1077 **Quando spiega la notte**
1078 **Sopra conca d'argento**
Cantate. Judith Nelson. HM 1010

ROSSINI, Gioacchino (1792-1868)
1079 **Les Adieux à la vie**
1080 **Arietta all'antica**
1081 **Chanson de Zora**
Serate musicali. Joan Sutherland. Lon OSA-13132
1082 **La danza**
Souvenirs. Elly Ameling. Col M 35119
Recital. Leyla Gencer. Cetra LPO 2003
Pavarotti in Concert. Luciano Pavarotti. Lon OS-26391
Songs. Renata Scotto. RCA V-AGLI 1-1341
1083 **Giovanna d'Arco**
Songs. Renata Scotto. RCA V-AGLI 1-1341
1084 **La gita in gondola**
Portrayals of Love in Italian Song. Anna Gabrieli. Orion ORA-78307
1085 **L'orgia**
Recital. Leyla Gencer. Cetra LPO 2003
1086 **La promessa**
Portrayals of Love in Italian Song. Anna Gabrieli. Orion ORA-78307
Recital. Leyla Gencer. Cetra LPO 2003
Recital of Songs and Arias. Renata Tebaldi. Lon R 23219

1087 Il rimprovero
       Portrayals of Love in Italian Song. Anna Gabrieli. Orion ORA-78307
1088 Soirées musicales
       Serate musicali. Joan Sutherland. Lon OSA-13132

RUBINSTEIN, Anton (1830-94)
1089 Es blinket der Tau
       Lieder der Schumannianer. Dietrich Fischer-Dieskau. Odeon
       C 06502673

SAINT-SAËNS, Camille (1835-1921)
1090 Aimons-nous
       Serate musicali. Joan Sutherland. Lon OSA-13132

SARRI, Domenico Natale (1679-1744)
1091 Sen corre l'agnelletta
       Arie amorose. Janet Baker. Phi 9500 557

SARTI, Giuseppe (1729-1802)
1092 Lungi dal caro bene
       Eighteenth Century Arias. Renata Tebaldi. Lon OS 26376
       Recital of Songs and Arias. Renata Tebaldi. Lon R 23219

SATIE, Erik (1866-1925)
1093 Chanson du chat (*Ludions*). *See also* **1099**
       Ravel and Satie. Régine Crespin. Col 36666
1094 Le Chapelier
1095 Daphénéo
       Ravel and Satie. Régine Crespin. Col 36666
       Erik Satie. Mady Mesplé. Ara 8053-L
       French Songs. Jessye Norman. Phi 9500 356
1096 La Diva de l'Empire
       Ein Liederabend. Elly Ameling. EMI 063-02375
       Ravel and Satie. Régine Crespin. Col 36666
       An Erik Satie Entertainment. Meriel Dickinson. Unicorn RHS 338
       Erik Satie. Mady Mesplé. Ara 8053-L
1097 Hymne: Salut Drapeau
       An Erik Satie Entertainment. Meriel Dickinson. Unicorn RHS 338
1098 Je te veux
       Ein Liederabend. Elly Ameling. EMI 063-02375
       Ravel and Satie. Régine Crespin. Col 36666
       An Erik Satie Entertainment. Meriel Dickinson. Unicorn RHS 338
       French Songs. Jessye Norman. Phi 9500 356

SATIE, Erik—*continued*
1099 **Ludions** (Air du rat; Spleen; La Grenouille américaine; Air du poète; Chanson du chat)
   Mélodies. Carol Kimball. Orion ORS 82422
1100 **L'Omnibus automobile**
   Ravel and Satie. Régine Crespin. Col 36666
1101 **Le Statue de bronze**
   Ravel and Satie. Régine Crespin. Col 36666
   French Songs. Jessye Norman. Phi 9500 356
1102 **Tendrement**
   Ravel and Satie. Régine Crespin. Col 36666
   An Erik Satie Entertainment. Meriel Dickinson. Unicorn RHS 338
1103 **Trois Autres Mélodies** (Chanson; Chanson médiévale; Les Fleurs)
1104 **Trois Mélodies** (Les Anges; Elégie; Sylvie)
   An Erik Satie Entertainment. Meriel Dickinson. Unicorn RHS 338
   Erik Satie. Mady Mesplé. Ara 8053-L

SCARLATTI, Alessandro (1660-1725)
1105 **Contentatevi, o fidi pensieri**
1106 **Dite almeno, astri crudeli**
   Scarlatti and Handel. Judith Blegen. Col M 34518
1107 **Già il sole dal Gange**
   Arie amorose. Janet Baker. Phi 9500 557
   Songs of the Italian Baroque. Carlo Berganzi. HNH 4008
   Pavarotti in Concert. Luciano Pavarotti. Lon OS 26391
1108 **Infelici miei lumi**
   Scarlatti and Handel. Judith Blegen. Col M 34518
1109 **O cessate di piagarmi**
   Songs of the Italian Baroque. Carlo Berganzi. HNH 4008
1110 **Se delitto è l'adorarti**
1111 **Se Florindo è fedele**
   Italian Baroque Songs. Teresa Berganza. DG 2531 192
1112 **Sento nel core**
   Arie amorose. Janet Baker. Phi 9500 557
1113 **Se tu della mia morte?**
   Von Stade Live. Frederica Von Stade. Col IM-37231
1114 **Spesso vibra per suo gioco**
   Arie amorose. Janet Baker. Phi 9500 557
1115 **Su le sponde del Tebro** (original version)
   Scarlatti and Handel. Judith Blegen. Col M 34518
1116 **Su, venite a consiglio**
1117 **Toglietemi la vita ancor**
   Songs of the Italian Baroque. Carlo Berganzi. HNH 4008

1118 **Tralascia pur di piangere**
Scarlatti and Handel. Judith Blegen. Col M 34518
1119 **Le violette**
Ein Liederabend. Elly Ameling. EMI C 063-02375
Italian Baroque Songs. Teresa Berganza. DG 2531 192
Songs of the Italian Baroque. Carlo Berganzi. HNH 4008
Eighteenth Century Arias. Renata Tebaldi. Lon OS 26376
Recital of Songs and Arias. Renata Tebaldi. Lon R 23219

SCHICKELE, Peter (b. 1935)
1120 **The Lowest Trees Have Tops** (Morning Song; The Lowest Trees Have
Tops; Hot Sun; My True-Love Hath My Heart; Noon Song; To Meadows;
The Mad Maid's Song; Evening Song; To Death)
The Jubal Trio. Lucy Shelton. Grenadilla GS 1015

SCHILLINGS, Max von (1868-1933)
1121 **Freude soll in deinen Werken sein**
Lieder der Neudeutschen. Dietrich Fischer-Dieskau. Odeon
C 06502674

SCHOECK, Othmar (1886-1957)
1122 **Abendwolken**
Lieder der Jahrhundertwende. Dietrich Fischer-Dieskau. Odeon
C 06502675
1123 **Peregrina**
Aufbruch des 20. Jahrhunderts im Lied. Dietrich Fischer-Dieskau.
Odeon C 06502676
1124 **Reiselied**
Lieder der Jahrhundertwende. Dietrich Fischer-Dieskau. Odeon
C 06502675

SCHOENBERG, Arnold (1874-1951)
1125 **Brettl-Lieder** (Galathea; Gigerlette; Der genügsame Liebhaber; Einfältiges
Lied; Mahnung; Jedem das Seine; Arie aus dem Spiegel von Arkadien;
Nachtwandler)
Cabaret Songs. Marni Nixon. RCA ARLI-1231
1126 **Das Buch der hängenden Gärten,** op. 15 (Unterm Schutz von dichten
Blättergründen; Hain in diesen Paradiesen; Als Neuling trat ich ein
in dein Gahege; Da meine Lippen reglos sind und brennen; Saget mir,
auf welchen Pfade; Jedem Werke bin ich fürder tot; Angst und Hoffen
wechselnd mich beklemenn; Wenn ich heut nicht Leib berühre;

SCHOENBERG, Arnold —*continued*
Streng ist uns das Glück und spröde; Das schöne Beet betracht ich mir
im Harren; Als wir hinter dem beblümten Tore; Wenn sich bei heiliger
Ruh; Du lehnest wider eine Silberweide; Sprich nicht immer; Wir
bevölkerten die Abend-düstern)
Schubert and Schoenberg. Jan De Gaetani. None H-71320
Debussy and Schoenberg. Charlotte Lehmann. EMI IC 165-46 356
1127 **Gigerlette** (*Brettl-Lieder*). See also **1125**
Souvenirs. Elly Ameling. Col M 35119
1128 **Herzgewächse**
Lieder. Dorothy Dorow. Tele 6,42350 AW
1129 **Nine Early Songs** (Mein Herz das ist ein tiefer Schacht; Ein Schilflied;
Mädchenlied; Mädchenfrühling; Die Beiden; Waldesnacht; Deinem Blick
mich zu bequemen; Gedenken; Nicht doch)
Cabaret Songs. Marni Nixon. RCA ARLI-1231
1130 **Traumleben**
1131 **Warnung**
Wirkung der neuen Wiener Schule im Lied. Dietrich Fischer-Dieskau.
Odeon C 06502677

SCHONTHAL, Ruth (b. 1924)
1132 **Totengesänge** (Totenglocken; Der ewige Liebe; Wiegenlied an ein
krankes Kind; Tod einer Jungfrau; Totentanz; Totenreigen; Hurenlied;
Die Spanierin)
Song Cycles for Soprano Plus. Berenice Bramson. Leonarda LPI 106

SCHREKER, Franz (1878-1934)
1133 **Die Dunkelheit sinkt schwer wie Blei**
Lieder der Jahrhundertwende. Dietrich Fischer-Dieskau.   Odeon
C 06502675

SCHUBERT, Franz (1797-1828)
1134 **Abendstern, D. 806**
Lieder Recital. Janet Baker. Odeon C 063-00391
Schubertiade. Judith Nelson. HM 1023/4
1135 **Abschied, D. 957** (*Schwanengesang*). See also **1240**
Schubert Lieder Recital. Hans Hotter. BWS IGI-386
Schubert Song Recital. Gerhard Hüsch. Ara 8107/3L
1136 **Alinde, D. 904**
Schubert Lieder Recital. Hans Hotter. BWS IGI-386

1137 **Die Allmacht,** D. 852
    Schubert and Strauss. Leontyne Price. Ang SZ-37631
1138 **Am Fenster,** D. 878
    Schubert Lieder. Dietrich Fischer-Dieskau. DG 2530 988
1139 **Am Grabe Anselmos,** D. 504
    Lieder Recital. Janet Baker. Odeon C 063-00391
1140 **Am Meer,** D. 957 *(Schwanengesang). See also* **1240**
    Schubert Song Recital. Gerhard Hüsch. Ara 8107/3L
1141 **An den Mond,** D. 296
    Lieder Recital. Julia Hamari. Hung SLPX-12406
    Schubert Lieder. Christa Ludwig. DG 2530 528
1142 **An den Tod,** D. 518
    Schubert Lieder Recital. Hans Hotter. BWS IGI-386
1143 **An die Laute,** D. 905
    Schubert Lieder. Elly Ameling. Phi 6500 704
    Schubert Lieder. Ian Partridge. Enigma VAR 1019
1144 **An die Musik,** D. 547
    Schubert and Brahms Lieder. Marian Anderson. RCA ARLI-3022
    Schubert Lieder Recital. Hans Hotter. BWS IGI-386
    Schubert Song Recital. Gerhard Hüsch. Ara 8107/3L
    Farewell Recital. Lotte Lehmann. Pel LP 2009
    Schubert Lieder. Ian Partridge. Enigma VAR 1019
1145 **An die Nachtigall,** D. 497
    Schubert and Schumann. Elly Ameling. Phi 6500 706
    German Songs. Benita Valente. Desmar DSM 1010
1146 **An mein Herz,** D. 860
    Schoenberg-Schubert. Jan De Gaetani. None H-71320
1147 **An Silvia,** D. 891
    Schubert Lieder. Elly Ameling. Phi 6500 704
    Schubert Lieder. Ian Partridge. Enigma VAR 1019
1148 **Atys,** D. 585
    Schubert Lieder Recital. Hans Hotter. BWS IGI-386
1149 **Auf dem Strom,** D. 943
    Schubert. Elly Ameling. Peters PLE 123
    Schubertiade. Judith Nelson. HM-1023/4
1150 **Auf der Bruck,** D. 853
1151 **Auf der Donau,** D. 553
    Schubert Lieder. Dietrich Fischer-Dieskau. DG 2530 988
1152 **Aufenthalt,** D. 957 *(Schwanengesang). See also* **1240**
    Lieder and Chansons. Gérard Souzay. Sera S-60251
1153 **Auflösung,** D. 807
    Lieder Recital. Janet Baker. Odeon C 063-00391
    Schubertiade. Judith Nelson. HM 1023/4
    Schubert Lieder. Ian Partridge. Enigma VAR 1019

SCHUBERT, Franz—*continued*
1154 **Aus "Heliopolis,"** D. 754
    Schubert Lieder. Dietrich Fischer-Dieskau. DG 2530 988
1155 **Ave Maria,** D. 839
    Schubert Songs. Elly Ameling. Phi 9500 169
    Schubertiade. Judith Nelson. HM 1023/4
    Schubert and Strauss. Leontyne Price. Ang SZ-37631
1156 **Bei dir allein,** D. 866
    Schubert Lieder. Ian Partridge. Enigma VAR 1019
1157 **Bertha's Lied in der Nacht,** D. 653
    Schubert Lieder. Christa Ludwig. DG 2530 528
1158 **Blondel zu Marien,** D. 626
    Schoenberg-Schubert. Jan De Gaetani. None H-71320
1159 **Der Blumenbrief,** D. 622
    Schubert Lieder. Elly Ameling. Phi 6500 704
1160 **Danksagung an den Bach,** D. 795 (*Die schöne Müllerin*). *See also* **1239**
    Farewell Recital. Lotte Lehmann. Pel LP 2009
1161 **Dass sie hier gewesen,** D. 775
    Schubert Lieder. Christa Ludwig. DG 2530 528
    Schubertiade. Judith Nelson. HM 1023/4
    Schubert Lieder. Ian Partridge. Enigma VAR 1019
1162 **Des Baches Wiegenlied,** D. 795 (*Die schöne Müllerin*). *See also* **1239**
    Farewell Recital. Lotte Lehmann. Pel LP 2009
1163 **Des Sängers Habe,** D. 832
    Schubert Lieder. Dietrich Fischer-Dieskau. DG 2530 988
    Schubert Lieder Recital. Hans Hotter. BWS IGI-386
1164 **Dithyrambe,** D. 801
    Recital. Elena Gerhardt. Disc KG-G-4
1165 **Der Doppelgänger,** D. 957 (*Schwanengesang).* *See also* **1240**
    Schubert Song Recital. Gerhard Hüsch. Ara 8107/3L
1166 **Du bist die Ruh,** D. 776
    German Romantic Songs. Elly Ameling. Phi 9500 350
1167 **Du liebst mich nicht,** D. 756
    Schubert Lieder. Elly Ameling. Phi 6500 704
1168 **Der Einsame,** D. 800
    Schubert Lieder. Elly Ameling. Phi 6500 704
    Schubert Lieder. Ian Partridge. Enigma VAR 1019
1169 **Ellens zweiter Gesang,** D. 838
    Recital. Elena Gerhardt. Disc KG-G-4
1170 **Erlkönig,** D. 328
    Schubert and Brahms Lieder. Marian Anderson. RCA ARLI-3022
    Lieder Recital. Julia Hamari. Hung SLPX-12406
    Ballads. Werner Hollweg. Tel 642620
    Schubert Song Recital. Gerhard Hüsch. Ara 8107/3L

1171 **Das Fischermädchen**, D. 957 (*Schwanengesang*). *See also* **1240**
Schubert Song Recital. Gerhard Hüsch. Ara 8107/3L
Lieder and Chansons. Gérard Souzay. Sera S-60251
1172 **Fischerweise**, D. 881
Schubert and Schumann. Elly Ameling. Phi 6500 706
Schubert Lieder. Dietrich Fischer-Dieskau. DG 2530 988
German Lieder. Marilyn Horne. Lon OS 26302
Schubert Lieder. Ian Partridge. Enigma VAR 1019
1173 **Die Forelle**, D. 550
Schubert and Brahms Lieder. Marian Anderson. RCA ARLI-3022
Schubertiade. Judith Nelson. HM 1023/4
Schubert Lieder. Ian Partridge. Enigma VAR 1019
1174 **Four Songs on Italian Texts**, D. 688 (Guarda, che bianca luna; Mio ben
ricordati; Non t'accostar all'urna; Da quel sembiante appresi)
Schubert. Elly Ameling. Peters PLE 123
1175 **Frühlingsglaube**, D. 686
Schubertiade. Judith Nelson. HM-1023/4
1176 **Ganymed**, D. 544
Schoenberg-Schubert. Jan De Gaetani. None H-71320
Schubert Lieder. Ian Partridge. Enigma VAR 1019
1177 **Die Gebüsche**, D. 646
Schubert and Schumann. Elly Ameling. Phi 6500 706
1178 **Geheimes**, D. 719
Schubert Lieder Recital. Hans Hotter. BWS IGI-386
1179 **Des Gondelfahrer**, D. 808
1180 **Die Götter Griechenlands**, D. 677
Lieder Recital. Janet Baker. Odeon C 063-00391
1181 **Griesengesang**, D. 778
Schubert Lieder Recital. Hans Hotter. BWS IGI-386
1182 **Gretchen am Spinnrade**, D. 118
Schubert Songs. Elly Ameling. Phi 9500 169
Schubert and Brahms Lieder. Marian Anderson. RCA ARLI-3022
Schubert and Strauss. Leontyne Price. Ang SZ 37631
Song Recital. Kiri Te Kanawa. Col M 36667
1183 **Gretchens Bitte**, D. 564
Schubert Songs. Elly Ameling. Phi 9500 169
1184 **Harfenspieler I**, D. 478
1185 **Harfenspieler III**, D. 480
Schubert Lieder Recital. Hans Hotter. BWS IGI-386
1186 **Heidenröslein**, D. 257
Schubert and Brahms Lieder. Marian Anderson. RCA ARLI-3022
Schoenberg-Schubert. Jan De Gaetani. None H-71320
Schubertiade. Judith Nelson. HM 1023/4
German Songs. Benita Valente. Desmar DSM 1010

SCHUBERT, Franz —*continued*
1187 **Herbst,** D. 945
    Schubert. Elly Ameling. Peters PLE 123
1188 **Der Hirt auf dem Felsen,** D. 965
    Schubert. Elly Ameling. Peters PLE 123
    The Ariel Ensemble. Julia Lovett. Orion 81411
    Schubertiade. Judith Nelson. HM 1023/4
    The Art of Elisabeth Schumann. Sera 60320
1189 **Ihr Bild,** D. 957 (*Schwanengesang*). *See also* **1240**
    Lieder and Chansons. Gérard Souzay. Sera S-60251
1190 **Im Abendrot,** D. 799
    Schubert Lieder. Elly Ameling. Phi 6500 704
1191 **Im Freien,** D. 880
    Schubert and Schumann. Elly Ameling. Phi 6500 706
1192 **Im Frühling,** D. 882
    Schubert Lieder. Dietrich Fischer-Dieskau. DG 2530 988
    German Lieder. Marilyn Horne. Lon OS-26302
    Schubertiade. Judith Nelson. HM 1023/4
1193 **Im Haine,** D. 738
    Schubert and Schumann. Elly Ameling. Phi 6500 706
1194 **In der Ferne,** D. 957 (*Schwanengesang*). *See also* **1240**
    Lieder and Chansons. Gérard Souzay. Sera S-60251
1195 **Jäger, ruhe von der Jagd,** D. 838. *See also* **1169**
    Schubert Songs. Elly Ameling. Phi 9500 169
1196 **Die junge Nonne,** D. 828
    Schubert Songs. Elly Ameling. Phi 9500 169
    German Lieder. Marilyn Horne. Lon OS 26302
    Schubert and Strauss. Leontyne Price. Ang SZ-37631
1197 **Klärchens Lied,** D. 210
    Schubert Lieder. Christa Ludwig. DG 2530 528
1198 **Der König in Thule,** D. 367
    Schubert Songs. Elly Ameling. Phi 9500 169
1199 **Der Kreuzzug,** D. 932
    Schubert Lieder Recital. Hans Hotter. BWS IGI-386
1200 **Lachen und Weinen,** D. 777
    Victoria de los Angeles in Concert. Ang SZ-37546
    Schubertiade. Judith Nelson. HM-1023/4
1201 **Die liebe Farbe,** D. 795 (*Die schöne Müllerin*). *See also* **1239**
    Farewell Recital. Lotte Lehmann. Pel LP 2009
1202 **Die Liebe hat gelogen,** D. 751
    Schubert Lieder. Elly Ameling. Phi 6500 704
    Schubert Lieder Recital. Hans Hotter. BWS IGI-386

1203 **Liebesbotschaft,** D. 957 (*Schwanengesang*). *See also* **1240**
   Schubert and Brahms Lieder. Marian Anderson. RCA ARLI-3022
   Schubertiade. Judith Nelson. HM 1023/4
   Schubert Lieder. Ian Partridge. Enigma VAR 1019
   Schubert and Strauss. Leontyne Price. Ang SZ-37631
1204 **Liebeslauschen,** D. 698
   Schubert Lieder. Dietrich Fischer-Dieskau. DG 2530 988
   Schubert Song Recital. Gerhard Hüsch. Ara 8107/3L
1205 **Der liebliche Stern,** D. 861
   Schubert Lieder. Elly Ameling. Phi 6500 704
1206 **Lied der Anna Lyle,** D. 830
   Schubert Lieder. Christa Ludwig. DG 2530 528
1207 **Lied der Mignon,** D. 877/4
   Schoenberg-Schubert. Jan De Gaetani. None H-71320
1208 **Lied der Mignon I,** D. 877/2
1209 **Lied der Mignon II,** D. 877/3
   Schubert Lieder. Christa Ludwig. DG 2530 528
1210 **Liedesend,** D. 473
   Schubert Lieder Recital. Hans Hotter. BWS IGI-386
1211 **Lied eines Schiffers an die Dioskuren,** D. 360
   Schubert Song Recital. Gerhard Hüsch. Ara 8107/3L
1212 **Das Lied im Grünen,** D. 907
   Schubert and Schumann. Elly Ameling. Phi 6500 706
1213 **Lilla an die Morgenröte,** D. 273
   Schubert Lieder. Christa Ludwig. DG 2530 528
1214 **Lob der Tränen,** D. 711
   Schubertiade. Judith Nelson. HM 1023/4
1215 **Loda's Gespenst,** D. 150
   Ballads. Werner Hollweg. Tele 642620
1216 **Das Mädchen,** D. 652
   Schubert Lieder. Elly Ameling. Phi 6500 704
   Schubert Lieder. Christa Ludwig. DG 2530 528
1217 **Die Männer sind méchant,** D. 866
   Schubert Lieder. Elly Ameling. Phi 6500 704
1218 **Meeres Stille,** D. 216
   Lieder Recital. Hans Hotter. BWS IGI-386
1219 **Mein,** D. 795 (*Die schöne Müllerin*). *See also* **1239**
   Victoria de los Angeles in Concert. Ang SZ-37546
1220 **Mignons Gesang,** D. 321
   Schubert Lieder. Christa Ludwig. DG 2530 528
1221 **Mignons Lied II,** D. 877. *See also* **1209**
   Schubert and Strauss. Leontyne Price. Ang SZ-37631

SCHUBERT, Franz—*continued*

1222 Minnelied, D. 429
    Schubert Lieder. Elly Ameling. Phi 6500 704
1223 Der Musensohn, D. 764
    Schoenberg-Schubert. Jan De Gaetani. None H-71320
    Lieder Recital. Julia Hamari. Hung SLPX-12406
    Schubert Song Recital. Gerhard Hüsch. Ara 8107/3L
1224 Nacht und Träume, D. 827
    Schubert Lieder. Elly Ameling. Phi 6500 704
    German Lieder. Marilyn Horne. Lon OS-26302
    Schubert and Strauss. Leontyne Price. Ang SZ-37631
    Song Recital. Kiri Te Kanawa. Col M-36667
    German Songs. Benita Valente. Desmar DSM 1010
1225 Nachtviolen, D. 752
    German Romantic Songs. Elly Ameling. Phi 9500 350
    Schubertiade. Judith Nelson. HM 1023/4
1226 Der Neugierige, D. 795 (*Die schöne Müllerin*). See also **1239**
    Farewell Recital. Lotte Lehmann. Pel LP 2009
1227 Orest und Tauris, D. 548
1228 Orpheus, D. 474
1229 Pilgerweise, D. 789
    Schubert Lieder Recital. Hans Hotter. BWS IGI-386
1230 Raste, Krieger, D. 837 (*Ellens Gesang I*)
    Schubert Songs. Elly Ameling. Phi 9500 169
    Schubertiade. Judith Nelson. HM 1023/4
1231 Rastlose Liebe, D. 138
    Schoenberg-Schubert. Jan De Gaetani. None H-71320
    Song Recital. Kiri Te Kanawa. Col M-36667
    German Songs. Benita Valente. Desmar DSM 1010
1232 Romance aus Rosamunde
    Schubert Lieder. Elly Ameling. Phi 6500 704
1233 Schäfers Klaglied, D. 121
    Schoenberg-Schubert. Jan De Gaetani. None H-71320
1234 Der Schäfer und der Reiter, D. 517
    Schubert Lieder Recital. Hans Hotter. BWS IGI-386
1235 Der Schiffer, D. 536
    Schubert Lieder. Dietrich Fischer-Dieskau. DG 2530 988
    Schubert Lieder. Ian Partridge. Enigma VAR 1019
1236 Schiffers Scheidelied, D. 910
    Schubert Lieder Recital. Hans Hotter. BWS IGI-386
1237 Schlummerlied, D. 527
    Schubert Lieder. Elly Ameling. Phi 6500 704

1238 Der Schmetterling, D. 633
    Schubert and Schumann. Elly Ameling. Phi 6500 706

1239 Die schöne Müllerin, D. 795 (Das Wandern; Wohin; Halt; Dangsagung
an den Bach; Am Feierabend; Der Neugierige; Ungeduld; Morgengruss;
Des Müllers Blumen; Thränenregen; Mein; Pause; Mit dem grünen
Lautenbande; Der Jäger; Eifersucht und Stolz; Die liebe Farbe; Die
böse Farbe; Trock'ne Blumen; Der Müller und der Bach; Des Baches
Wiegenlied)
    Dietrich Fischer-Dieskau. DG 2530 544
    Grayson Hirst. Leonarda LPI 112
    Gerhard Hüsch. Ara 8107/3L

1240 Schwanengesang, D. 957 (Liebesbotschaft; Kriegers Ahnung;
Frühlingssehnsucht; Ständchen; Aufenthalt; In der Ferne; Abschied;
Der Atlas; Ihr Bild; Das Fischermädchen; Die Stadt; Am Meer;
Der Doppelgänger; Die Taubenpost)
    Schubert. Hermann Prey. DG 2531 235

1241 Sehnsucht, D. 636b
    Schubert Lieder. Christa Ludwig. DG 2530 528

1242 Seligkeit, D. 433
    Ein Liederabend. Elly Ameling. EMI 063-02375
    Schubert Lieder. Elly Ameling. Phi 6500 704
    Schubertiade. Judith Nelson. HM 1023/4

1243 Die Sommernacht, D. 289b
    Schubert. Elly Ameling. Peters PLE 123

1244 Sprache der Liebe, D. 410
    Schoenberg-Schubert. Jan De Gaetani. None H-71320

1245 Die Stadt, D. 957 (*Schwanengesang*). *See also* **1240**
    Recital. Elena Gerhardt. Disc KG-G-4

1246 Ständchen, D. 889 (Horch, horch, die Lerch)
    Schubert Song Recital. Gerhard Hüsch. Ara 8107/3L

1247 Ständchen, D. 921 (Zögernd leise)
    Schubert Lieder. Christa Ludwig. DG 2530 528

1248 Ständchen, D. 957 (*Schwanengesang*). *See also* **1240**
    Schubert Song Recital. Gerhard Hüsch. Ara 8107/3L
    Schubert Lieder. Ian Partridge. Enigma VAR 1019

1249 Die Sterne, D. 939
    Schubert Lieder. Elly Ameling. Phi 6500 704
    Schubert Lieder. Dietrich Fischer-Dieskau. DG 2530 988
    Schubert Lieder. Ian Partridge. Enigma VAR 1019

1250 Der Strom, D. 565
    Schubert Lieder. Dietrich Fischer-Dieskau. DG 2530 988

SCHUBERT, Franz—*continued*

1251 Suleika, D. 720
    Schubert Songs. Elly Ameling. Phi 9500 169
    Schubert and Brahms Lieder. Marian Anderson. RCA ARLI-3022
    Schubertiade. Judith Nelson. HM-1023/4

1252 Suleikas zweiter Gesang, D. 717
    Schubert Songs. Ely Ameling. Phi 9500 169
    Schubertiade. Judith Nelson. HM-1023/4

1253 Die Taubenpost, D. 957 (*Schwanengesang*). *See also* **1240**
    Schubert Song Recital. Gerhard Hüsch. Ara 8107/3L

1254 Tiefes Lied, D. 876
    Schubert Lieder Recital. Hans Hotter. BWS IGI-386

1255 Totengräbers Heimweh, D. 842
    Schubert Lieder. Dietrich Fischer-Dieskau. DG 2530 988
    Schubert Lieder Recital. Hans Hotter. BWS IGI-386

1256 Der Tod und das Mädchen, D. 531
    Schubert and Brahms Lieder. Marian Anderson. RCA ARLI-3022

1257 Tränenregen, D. 795 (*Die schöne Müllerin*). *See also* **1239**
    Farewell Recital. Lotte Lehmann. Pel LP 2009

1258 Über Wildemann, D. 884
    Schubert Lieder. Ian Partridge. Enigma VAR 1019

1259 Ungeduld, D. 795 (*Die schöne Müllerin*). *See also* **1239**
    Schubert and Brahms Lieder. Marian Anderson. RCA ARLI-3022

1260 Die Vögel, D. 691
    Schubert and Schumann. Elly Ameling. Phi 6500 706
    Lieder Recital. Janet Baker. Odeon C 063-00391

1261 Der Wachtelschlag, D. 742
    Schubert and Schumann. Elly Ameling. Phi 6500 706

1262 Der Wanderer, D. 649
    Schubert Lieder. Dietrich Fischer-Dieskau. DG 2530 988
    Schubert Lieder Recital. Hans Hotter. BWS IGI-386
    Schubert Song Recital. Gerhard Hüsch. Ara 8107/3L

1263 Der Wanderer an den Mond, D. 870
    Schubert Lieder. Ian Partridge. Enigma VAR 1019

1264 Wanderers Nachtlied, D. 224
    Schubert Lieder Recital. Hans Hotter. BWS IGI-386
    Schubert Lieder. Ian Partridge. Enigma VAR 1019

1265 Wehmut, D. 772
    Schubert Lieder. Dietrich Fischer-Dieskau. DG 2530 988
    Schubert Lieder. Christa Ludwig. DG 2530 528

1266 Wer nie sein Brot mit Tränen ass, D. 480. *See also* **1185**

1267 Wer sich der Einsamkeit ergibt, D. 325 (Harfenspieler)
    Schubert Song Recital. Gerhard Hüsch. Ara 8107/3L

1268 **Westwind Song.** *See* **1252**
1269 **Widerschein,** D. 949
  Schubert Song Recital. Gerhard Hüsch. Ara 8107/3L
1270 **Wiegenlied,** D. 498
  Schubert and Brahms Lieder. Marian Anderson. RCA ARLI-3022
  Recital. Elena Gerhardt. Disc KG-G-4
1271 **Der Winterabend,** D. 938
  Schubert. Elly Ameling. Peters PLE 123
1272 **Die Winterreise,** D. 911 (Gute Nacht; Die Wetterfane; Gefrorne Thränen;
  Erstarrung; Der Lindenbaum; Wasserfluth; Auf dem Flusse; Rückblick;
  Irrlicht; Rast; Frühlingstraum; Einsamkeit; Die Post; Der greise Kopf; Die
  Krähe; Letzte Hoffnung; Im Dorfe; Der stürmische Morgen; Täuschung;
  Der Wegweiser; Das Wirtshaus; Muth; Die Nebensonnen; Der Leiermann)
  Dietrich Fischer-Dieskau. DG 3301 237
  Schubert Song Recital. Gerhard Hüsch. Ara 8107/3L
1273 **Wohin,** D. 795 (*Die schöne Müllerin*). *See also* **1239**
  Farewell Recital. Lotte Lehmann. Pel LP 2009
1274 **Das Zügenglöcklein,** D. 871
  Schubert Lieder. Dietrich Fischer-Dieskau. DG 2530 988
  Schubert Lieder Recital. Hans Hotter. BWS IGI-386
1275 **Der Zwerg,** D. 771
  Ballads. Werner Hollweg. Tele 642620
  Schubert Lieder. Christa Ludwig. DG 2530 528

SCHUMAN, William (b. 1910)
1276 **In Sweet Music**
1277 **Time to the Old** (The Old Gray Couple; Conway Burying Ground; Dozing
  on the Lawn)
1278 **The Young Dead Soldiers**
  William Schuman. Rosalind Rees. CRI SD 439

SCHUMANN, Clara (1819-96)
1279 **Das ist ein Tag, der klingen mag**
1280 **Er ist gekommen in Sturm und Regen**
1281 **Ich stand in dunklen Träumen**
1282 **Liebst du um Schönheit**
1283 **Die stille Lotusblume**
1284 **Warum willst du And're tragen**
1285 **Was weinst du, Blümlein**
  Lieder. Katherine Ciesinski. Leonarda LPI 107

SCHUMANN, Robert (1810-56)
1286 Schumann Lieder, volume I
    Liederkreis, op. 25 (excerpts)
        Widmung; Freisinn; Der Nussbaum; Sitz'ich allein; Setze mir nicht;
        Die Lotusblume; Talismane; Hochländers Abschied; Mein Herz
        ist schwer; Rätsel; Zwei Venezianische Lieder; Hauptmanns
        Weib; Was will die einsame Träne; Niemand; Du bist wie eine
        Blume; Aus den östlichen Rosen; Zum Schluss
    Lieder und Gesänge, op. 27
        Sag an, o lieber Vogel mein; Dem roten Röslein gleicht mein Lieb;
        Was soll ich sagen?; Jasminenstrauch; Nur ein lächelnder Blick
    Drei Gedichte, op. 30
        Der Knabe mit dem Wunderhorn; Der Page; Der Hidalgo
    Drei Gesänge, op. 31 (excerpts)
        Die Löwenbraut; Die rote Hanne
    Aus dem Liederbuch eines Malers, op. 36
        Sonntags am Rhein; Ständchen; Nichts Schöneres; An den
        Sonnenschein; Dichters Genesung; Liebesbotschaft
    Zwölf Gedichte aus Rückerts ''Liebesfrühling,'' op. 37 (excerpts)
        Der Himmel hat eine Träne geweint; Ich hab'in mich gesogen;
        Flügel, Flugel, um zu fliegen, Rose, Meer und Sonne
    Liederkreis, op. 39
    Fünf Lieder, op. 40
        Märzveilchen; Muttertraum; Der Soldat; Der Spielmann;
        Verratene Liebe
    Romanzen und Balladen, op. 45 (excerpts)
        Der Schatzgräber; Frühlingsfahrt
    Der frohe Wandersmann, op. 77/1
    Schumann Lieder, volume I. Dietrich Fischer-Dieskau. DG 2709 074
1287 Schumann Lieder, volume II
    Liederkreis, op. 24
    Zwölf Gedichte (*Kerner Lieder*), op. 35
    Abends am Strand, op. 45/3
    Dichterliebe, op. 48
    Romanzen und Balladen, op. 49
        Die beiden Grenadiere; Die feindlichen Brüder
    Auf dem Rhein, op. 51/4
    Romanzen und Balladen, op. 53
        Loreley; Der arme Peter I, II, III
    Belsatzar, op. 57
    Tragödie I, II, op. 64/3a, b
    Aus dem Zyklus ''Spanisches Liederbuch,'' op. 74 (excerpts)
        Malencholie; Geständnis; Der Contrabandiste
    Aufträge, op. 77/5

Liederalbum für die Jugend, op. 79 (excerpts)
Zigeunerliedchen, no. 7; Zigeunerliedchen, no. 8; Marienwürm-
chen; Die wandelnde Glocke; Des Sennin Abschied; Er ists;
Schneeglöckchen; Lynceus des Türmers
Schumann Lieder, volume II. Dietrich Fischer-Dieskau. DG 2709 079
1288 **Schumann Lieder,** volume III
Drei Gesänge, op. 83 (excerpts)
Resignation; Der Einseidler
Sechs Gesänge, op. 89 (excerpts)
Es stürmet am Abendhimmel; Heimliches Verschwinden;
Herbstlied; Abschied vom Walde; Ins Freie
Sechs Gedichte von Nikolaus Lenau and **Requiem** (Anhang, Nr. 7),
op. 90
Lied eines Schmiedes; Meine Rose; Kommen und Scheiden; Die
Sennin; Einsamkeit; Der schwere Abend; Requiem
An den Mond, op. 95/2:
Lieder und Gesänge, op. 96 (excerpts)
Nachtlied; Schneeglöckchen; Ihre Stimme
Lieder und Gesänge, op. 98a (excerpts)
Ballade des Harfners; Wer nie sein Brot mit Tränen ass; Wer sich
der Einsamkeit ergibt; An die Türen will ich schleichen
Mein schöner Stern, op. 104/4
Schöne Hedwig, op.106
Sechs Gesänge, op. 107 (excerpts)
Der Gärtner; Abendlied
Vier Husarenlieder, op. 117
Der Husar; Der leidige Frieden; Den grünen Zeigern; Da liegt der
Feinde gestreckte Schar
Warnung, op. 119/2
Zwei Balladen, op. 122
Vom Heideknaben; Die Flüchtlinge
Fünf heitere Gesänge, op. 125 (excerpts)
Die Meerfee; Husarenabzug; Jung Volkers Lied
Fünf Lieder und Gesänge, op. 127 (excerpts)
Dein Angesicht; Es leuchtet meine Liebe
Aus dem Zyklus "Spanisches Liebeslieder," op. 138
Tief im Herzen trag'ich Pein; O wie lieblich ist das Mädchen;
Romanze; Weh, wie zornig ist das Mädchen
Provencalisches Lied, op. 139/4
Vier Gesänge, op. 142 (excerpts)
Trost im Gesang; Lehn deine Wang'; Mein Wagen rollet langsam
Sechs frühe Lieder, op. post. (Wo O 21)
Sehnsucht; Die Weinende; Erinnerung; Kurzes Erwachen;
Gesanges Erwachen; An Anna
Schumann Lieder, volume III. Dietrich Fischer-Dieskau. DG 2709 088

SCHUMANN, Robert—*continued*

1289 Liederkreis, op. 24 (Morgens steh'ich auf und frage; Es treibt mich hin; Ich wandelte unter den Bäumen; Lieb' Liebchen, leg's Händchen; Schöne Wiege meiner Leiden; Warte, warte, wilder Schiffsmann; Berg' und Burgen schau'n herunter; Anfangs wollt' ich fast verzagen; Mit Myrthen und Rosen)

> *Schumann Lieder,* volume III. Dietrich Fischer-Dieskau. DG 2530 543

1290 Myrthen, op. 25 (excerpts) (Aus den hebräischen Gesängen; Aus den östlichen Rosen; Du bist wie eine Blume; Freisinn; Hauptmanns Weib; Hochländers Abschied; Die Lotusblume; Niemand; Der Nussbaum; Rätsel; Setze mir nicht; Sitz ich allein; Talismane; Venezianisches Lied I, II; Was will die einsame Träne; Widmung; Zum Schluss)

> *Schumann Lieder,* volume III. Dietrich Fischer-Dieskau. DG 2530 543

1291 Zwölf Gedichte, op. 35 (*Kerner Lieder*) (Lust der Sturmnacht; Stirb, Lieb' und Freud; Wanderlied; Erstes Grün; Sehnsucht nach der Waldgegend; Auf das Trinkglas eines verstorbenen Freundes; Wanderung; Stille Liebe; Frage; Stille Tränen; Wer machte dich so krank?; Alte Laute)

> *Schumann.* Gérard Souzay. Roc 5372

1292 Liederkreis, op. 39 (In der Fremde; Intermezzo; Waldesgespräch; Die Stille; Mondnacht; Schöne Fremde; Auf einer Burg; Wehmut; Zwielicht; Im Walde; Frühlingsnacht)

> *Schumann.* Elly Ameling. Phi 6769 037
> *Schumann.* Janet Baker. Ang S-37222
> *Schumann.* Dietrich Fischer-Dieskau. DG 2531 290
> *Schumann.* Jessye Norman. Phi 9500 110
> *Schumann.* Elisabeth Schwarzkopf. Ang S-37043

1293 Fünf Lieder, op. 40 (Märzveilchen; Muttertraum; Der Soldat; Der Spielmann; Verratene Liebe)

> *Schumann.* Peter Schreier. RCA RL 25126

1294 Frauenliebe und Leben, op. 42 (Seit ich ihn gesehen; Er, der Herrlichste von allen; Ich kanns nicht fassen; Du Ring an meinem Finger; Helft mir, ihr Schwestern; Süsser Freund, du blickest; An meinem Herzen; Nun hast du mir den ersten Schmerz)

> *Schumann and Schubert.* Elly Ameling. Phi 6500 706
> *Schumann.* Janet Baker. Ang S-37222
> *Schumann.* Edith Mathis. DG 2531 323
> *Schumann.* Jessye Norman. Phi 9500 110
> *Robert Schumann.* Lucia Popp. Euro 201 298 366
> *Schumann.* Elisabeth Schwarzkopf. Ang S-37043

1295 Dichterliebe, op. 48 (Im wunderschönen Monat Mai; Aus meinen Tränen spriessen; Die Rose, die Lilie; Wenn ich in deine Augen seh; Ich will meine Seele tauchen; Im Rhein, im heiligen Strome; Ich grolle nicht; Und wüsstens die Blumen; Das is ein Flöten und Geigen;

Hör ich das Liedchen klingen; Ein Jüngling liebt ein Mädchen; Am
leuchtenden Sommermorgen; Ich hab im Traum geweinet; Allnächtlich
im Traume; Aus alten Märchen; Die alten, bösen Lieder)
Schumann. Dietrich Fischer-Dieskau. DG 2531 290
Schumann. Gérard Souzay. Roc 5372

1296 **Liederalbum für die Jugend,** op. 79 (Der Abendstern; Schmetterling;
Frühlingsbotschaft; Frühlingsgruss; Vom Schlaraffenland; Sonntag;
Zigeunerliedchen I, II; Des Knaben Berglied; Mailied; Käuzlein; Hinaus
ins Freie; Der Sandmann; Marienwürmchen; Die Waise; Das Gluck;
Weinachtslied; Die wandelnde Glocke; Frühlingslied; Frühlingsankunft; Die
Schwalben; Kinderwacht; Des Sennen Abschied; Er ist's; Spinnlied; Des
Buben Schützenlied; Schneeglöckchen; Lied Lynceus des Türmers; Mignon)
Schumann. Elly Ameling. Phi 6769 037

1297 **Sechs Gedichte,** op. 90 (Lied eines Schmiedes; Meine Rose; Kommen
und Scheiden; Die Sennin; Einsamkeit; Der schwere Abend)
Schumann. Peter Schreier. RCA RL 25126

1298 **Abendlied,** op. 106/6
Elly Ameling singt Lieder von Robert Schumann. Odeon C 06302184
German Lieder. Marilyn Horne. Lon OS-26302

1299 **Alte Laute,** op. 35/12
Farewell Recital. Lotte Lehmann. Pel LP 2009

1300 **An den Mond,** op. 95/2

1301 **Der arme Peter,** op. 53/3
Schumann. Peter Schreier. RCA RL 25126

1302 **Aufträge,** op. 77/5
Elly Ameling singt Lieder von Robert Schumann. Odeon C 06302184
Schumann. Peter Schreier. RCA RL 25126

1303 **Aus den hebräischen Gesängen,** op. 25/15
German Lieder. Marilyn Horne. Lon OS-26302

1304 **Aus den östlichen Rosen,** op. 25/25
Schumann. Peter Schreier. RCA RL 25126

1305 **Die beiden Grenadiere,** op. 49/1

1306 **Belsatzar,** op. 57
Ballads. Werner Hollweg. Tele 642620

1307 **Die Blume der Ergebung,** op. 83/2
Schumann. Edith Mathis. DG 2531 323

1308 **Du bist wie eine Blume,** op. 25/24
Song Recital. Kiri Te Kanawa. Col M 36667

1309 **Er ist's,** op. 79/24

1310 **Erstes Grün,** op. 35/4
Robert Schumann. Lucia Popp. Euro 201 298 366

1311 **Die feindlichen Brüder,** op. 49/2
Ballads. Werner Hollweg. Tele 642620

SCHUMANN, Robert—*continued*
1312 Freisinn, op. 25/2
1313 Frühlingsfahrt, op. 45/2
    Schumann. Peter Schreier. RCA RL 25126
1314 Frühlingsgruss, op. 79/4
    Robert Schumann. Lucia Popp. Euro 201 298 366
1315 Frühlingslust, op. 125/5
    Schumann. Edith Mathis. DG 2531 323
    Robert Schumann. Lucia Popp. Euro 201 298 366
1316 Geisternähe, op. 77/3
    Elly Ameling singt Lieder von Robert Schumann. Odeon C 06302184
    Schumann. Peter Schreier. RCA RL 25126
1317 Geständnis, op. 74/7
    Schumann. Peter Schreier. RCA RL 25126
1318 Herzeleid, op. 107/1
    Elly Ameling singt Lieder von Robert Schumann. Odeon C 06302184
1319 Der Hidalgo, op. 30/3
    Schumann. Peter Schreier. RCA RL 25126
1320 Der Himmel hat eine Träne geweint, op. 37/1
    Elly Ameling singt Lieder von Robert Schumann. Odeon C 06302184
1321 Hinaus ins Freie, op. 79/12
    Schumann. Edith Mathis. DG 2531 323
1322 Jasminenstrauch, op. 27/4
    Elly Ameling singt Lieder von Robert Schumann. Odeon C 06302184
    Schumann. Peter Schreier. RCA RL 25126
1323 Der Knabe mit dem Wunderhorn, op. 30/1
    Schumann. Peter Schreier. RCA RL 25126
1324 Die Kartenlegerin, op. 31/2
    Elly Ameling singt Lieder von Robert Schumann. Odeon C 06302184
    German Lieder. Marilyn Horne. Lon OS-26302
1325 Kinderwacht, op. 79/22
    Schumann. Edith Mathis. DG 2531 323
1326 Leis' rudern hier (*Venezianisches Lied I*), op. 25/17
    Schumann. Peter Schreier. RCA RL 25126
1327 Die letzten Blumen, op. 104/6
    Schumann. Edith Mathis. DG 2531 323
1328 Liebeslied, op. 51/5
1329 Lied der Suleika, op. 25/9
    Elly Ameling singt Lieder von Robert Schumann. Odeon C 06302184
    Schumann. Edith Mathis. DG 2531 323
1330 Loreley, op. 53/2
    Elly Ameling singt Lieder von Robert Schumann. Odeon C 06302184
    Schumann. Peter Schreier. RCA RL 25126

1331 **Die Lotusblume,** op. 25/7
 Elly Ameling singt Lieder von Robert Schumann. Odeon C 06302184
 German Lieder. Marilyn Horne. Lon OS-26302
1332 **Lust der Sturmnacht,** op. 35/1
 Lieder and Chansons. Gérard Souzay. Sera S-60251
1333 **Mädchen-Schwermut,** op. 142/3
1334 **Marienwürmchen,** op. 79/14
1335 **Meine Töne still und heiter,** 101/1
 Schumann. Peter Schreier. RCA RL 25126
1336 **Mein Garten,** op. 77/2
 Robert Schumann. Lucia Popp. Euro 201 298 366
1337 **Mein schöner Stern,** op. 101/4
 Schumann. Peter Schreier. RCA RL 25126
 Lieder and Chansons. Gérard Souzay. Sera S-60251
1338 **Melancholie,** op. 74/6
 Elly Ameling singt Lieder von Robert Schumann. Odeon C 06302184
1339 **Mignon** (Kennst du das Land), op. 79/29
 Robert Schumann. Lucia Popp. Euro 201 298 366
1340 **Mignon,** op. 98a/4
 Strauss and Schumann. Edda Moser. Elec 1C 065-45 418
1341 **Mignon** (Heiss' mich nicht reden), op. 98a/8
 Elly Ameling singt Lieder von Robert Schumann. Odeon C 06302184
 Strauss and Schumann. Edda Moser. Elec 1C 065-45 418
1342 **Mit Myrten und Rosen,** op. 24/9
 Robert Schumann. Lucia Popp. Euro 201 298 366
1343 **Mond, meiner Seele Liebling,** op. 104/1
 Schumann. Edith Mathis. DG 2531 323
1344 **Nur ein lächender Blick,** op. 27/5
 Schumann. Peter Schreier. RCA RL 25126
1345 **Nur wer die Sehnsucht kennt** (Lied der Mignon), op. 98a/5
 Strauss and Schumann. Edda Moser. Elec 1C 065-45 418
1346 **Der Nussbaum,** op. 25/3
 Elly Ameling singt Lieder von Robert Schumann. Odeon C 06302184
 German Romantic Songs. Elly Ameling. Phi 9500 350
1347 **Oh, ihr Herren,** op. 37/3
 Farewell Recital. Lotte Lehmann. Pel LP 2009
1348 **O, wie lieblich ist das Mädchen,** op. 138/7
1349 **Der Page,** op. 30/2
 Schumann. Peter Schreier. RCA RL 25126
1350 **Philine,** op. 98a/7
 Elly Ameling singt Lieder von Robert Schumann. Odeon C 06302184
1351 **Reich mir die Hand,** op. 104/5
 Schumann. Edith Mathis. DG 2531 323
 Robert Schumann. Lucia Popp. Euro 201 298 366

SCHUMANN, Robert—*continued*

1352 **Requiem,** op. 90/7
    Strauss and Schumann. Edda Moser. Elec 1C 065-45 418
    Schumann. Peter Schreier. RCA RL 25126

1353 **Resignation,** op. 83/1
    Elly Ameling singt Lieder von Robert Schumann. Odeon C 06302184

1354 **Romanze,** op. 138/5
    Schumann. Peter Schreier. RCA RL 25126

1355 **Röselein, Röselein,** op. 89/6
    Robert Schumann. Lucia Popp. Euro 201 298 366

1356 **Der Sandmann,** op. 79/13

1357 **Schmetterling,** op. 79/2
    Schumann. Edith Mathis. DG 2531 232

1358 **Schneeglöckchen,** op. 79/27
    Robert Schumann. Lucia Popp. Euro 201 298 366

1359 **Sehnsucht,** op. 51/1

1360 **Setze mir nicht,** op. 25/6
    Schumann. Peter Schreier. RCA RL 25126

1361 **Singet nicht in Trauertönen,** op. 98a/7
    Schumann. Edith Mathis. DG 2531 323
    Strauss and Schumann. Edda Moser. Elec 1C 065-45 418

1362 **Sitz' ich allein,** op. 25/5
    Schumann. Peter Schreier. RCA RL 25126

1363 **So lasst mich scheinen, bis ich werde,** op. 98a/9
    Strauss and Schumann. Edda Moser. Elec 1C 065-45 418

1364 **Der Soldat,** op. 40/3
    Ballads. Werner Hollweg. Tele 642620

1365 **Die Soldatenbraut,** op. 64/1
    Elly Ameling singt Lieder von Robert Schumann. Odeon C 06502184
    Song Recital. Kiri Te Kanawa. Col M 36667

1366 **So sei gegrüsst viel tausendmal,** op. 79/4
    Schumann. Peter Schreier. RCA RL 25126

1367 **Ständchen,** op. 36/2
    Farewell Recital. Lotte Lehmann. Pel LP 2009
    Schumann. Peter Schreier. RCA RL 25126

1368 **Stille Liebe,** op. 35/8
    Lieder and Chansons. Gërard Souzay. Sera S-60251

1369 **Stiller Vorwurf,** op. 77/4
    Elly Ameling singt Lieder von Robert Schumann. Odeon C 06302184

1370 **Stille Tränen,** op. 35/10
    Strauss and Schumann. Edda Moser. Elec 1C 065-45 418
    Lieder and Chansons. Gérard Souzay. Sera S-60251
    Song Recital. Kiri Te Kanawa. Col M 36667

1371 **Talismane,** op. 25/8
    Schumann. Peter Schreier. RCA RL 25126
1372 **Volksliedchen,** op. 51/2
    Elly Ameling singt Lieder von Robert Schumann. Odeon C 06302184
1373 **Die wandelnde Glocke,** op. 79/18
    Ballads. Werner Hollweg. Tel 642620
1374 **Wanderers Nachtlied,** op. 96/1
1375 **Weh, wie zornig ist das Mädchen,** op. 138
    Schumann. Peter Schreier. RCA RL 25126
1376 **Weit! Weit!,** op. 25/20
    Schumann. Edith Mathis. DG 2531 323
1377 **Wenn durch die Piazetta,** op. 25/18
    Schumann. Peter Schreier. RCA RL 25126
1378 **Widmung,** op. 25/1
    Elly Ameling singt Lieder von Robert Schumann. Odeon C 06302184
    German Romantic Songs. Elly Ameling. Phi 9500 350
    Farewell Recital. Lotte Lehmann. Pel LP 2009
    Schumann. Peter Schreier. RCA RL 25126
    Lieder and Chansons. Gérard Souzay. Sera S-60251
1379 **Zigeunerliedchen,** op. 79/7
1380 **Zum Schloss,** op. 25/26
    Schumann. Peter Schreier. RCA RL 25126

SCOTT, Lady John (Alicia Ann) (1810-1900)
1381 **Think on Me**
    Think on Me. Elly Ameling. CBS 26682

SEIBER, Matyas (1905-60)
1382 **Four French Folk Songs** (Réveillez-vous; J'ai descendu; Le Rossignol;
    Marguerite, elle est malade)
    Music for Voice and Guitar. Peter Pears. RCA V-AGLI-1281

SESSIONS, Roger (b. 1896)
1383 **On the Beach at Fontana**
    But Yesterday Is Not Today. Bethany Beardslee. NW 243

SHIELDS, Alice Ferree (b. 1943)
1384 **Wildcat Songs**
    Recital. Stephanie Turash. Opus One 13

SHOSTAKOVICH, Dmitri (1906-75)
1385 **Satires** (Pictures of the Past), op. 109 (To a Critic; Taste of Spring; Progeny; Misunderstanding; Kreutzer Sonata)
1386 **Seven Poems,** op. 127 (Song of Ophelia; Gamayun, Bird of Prophecy; We Were Together; The City Sleeps; Storm; Secret Signs; Music)
Russian Songs. Galina Vishnevskaya. EMI SLS 5055

SIBELIUS, Jean (1865-1957)
1387 **Varn flyktar hastigt**
Souvenirs. Elly Ameling. Col M 35119

SIEGMEISTER, Elie (b. 1909)
1388 **Songs of Experience** (The Voice of the Bard; Earth's Answer; The Fly; The Garden of Love; The Thief and the Lady; The Tyger)
The Cantilena Chamber Players. Elaine Bonazzi. Grenadilla GS-1029/30

SIMON, Louis-Victor
1389 **Il pleut bergère**
Bergerettes et Pastourelles. Mady Mesplé. Pathé 2C 069-14044

SMETANA, Bedřich (1824-84)
1390 **Cradle Song**
The Art of Elisabeth Schumann. Sera 60320

SMIT, Leo (b. 1921)
1391 **Songs of Wonder** (Untold Wonders; The Horizons of Time; A Magic Starry Night)
Other Voices. Martha Hanneman. CRI SD 370

SNYDER, Leo (b. 1918)
1392 **Love Is a Language** (Language Is a Language; Speak Out in the Night; In the Manner of Candles; A Bed's a Small Domain; Uneasy Lies My King Abed; Justify This Grief)
Love Can Be Still. Elena Gambulos. NR 201

SPIES, Claudio (b. 1925)
1393 **Three Songs on Poems by May Swenson** (Came a Beauty; Living Tenderly; The Woods at Night)
Music by Claudio Spies. Christine Whittlesey. CRI SD 445

STARER, Robert (b. 1924)
1394 **Anna Margarita's Will**
   Starer and Perlongo. Phyllis Bryn-Julson. CRI 453
1395 **The Ideal Self**
   The Ariel Ensemble. Julia Lovett. Orion 81411

STRADELLA, Alessandro (ca. 1645-82)
1396 **Ragion sempre addita**
   Arie amorose. Janet Baker. Phi 9500 557

STRAUSS, Richard (1864-1949)
1397 **Ach Lieb, ich muss nun scheiden,** op. 21/3
1398 **Ach weh mir unglückhaftem Mann,** op. 21/4
   Strauss Lieder. Bernd Weikl. DG 2531 076
1399 **Allerseelen,** op. 10/8
   German Romantic Songs. Elly Ameling. Phi 9500 350
   Lieder Recital. Janet Baker. Odeon C 063 00391
   Lieder Recital. Julia Hamari. Hung SLPX-12406
1400 **All' mein Gedanken,** op. 21/1
   Lieder Recital. Janet Baker. Odeon C 063-00391
1401 **Als mir dein Lied erklang,** op. 68/4
   Song Recital. Montserrat Caballé. Ang SZB-3903
   Strauss Songs. Hilde Gueden. Lon 23212
   Schubert and Strauss. Leontyne Price. Ang SZ-37631
1402 **Amor,** op. 68/5
   Strauss and Wolf. Judith Blegen. RCA ARLI-1571
1403 **Am Ufer,** op. 41a/3
   Strauss Songs. Helen-Kay Eberley. Eb-Sko ES-1005
1404 **Befreit,** op. 39/4
   Lieder Recital. Janet Baker. Odeon C 063 00391
   Strauss Songs. Helen-Kay Eberley. Eb-Sko ES-1005
   Strauss Songs. Hilde Gueden. Lon 23212
   German Lieder. Marilyn Horne. Lon OS-26302
   Strauss and Schumann. Edda Moser. Elec 1C 065-45 418
   Schubert and Strauss. Leontyne Price. Ang SZ-37631
   Strauss. Kiri Te Kanawa. Col M-35140
1405 **Breit' über mein Haupt,** op. 19/2
   Strauss Songs. Helen-Kay Eberley. Eb-Sko ES-1005
   Schubert and Strauss. Leontyne Price. Ang SZ-37631
   Strauss Lieder. Bernd Weikl. DG 2531 076

STRAUSS, Richard—*continued*
1406 **Cäcilie**, op. 27/2
    Schubert and Strauss. Leontyne Price. Ang SZ-37631
    Strauss Song Recital. Sylvia Sass. Hung SLPX-12397
    Strauss Lieder. Bernd Weikl. DG 2531 076
1407 **Des Dichters Abendgang,** op. 47/2
    Song Recital. Montserrat Caballé. Ang SZB-3903
1408 **Drei Lieder der Ophelia aus "Hamlet",** op. 67 (Wie erkenn ich mein Treulich vor andern nun; Guten Morgen, 's ist Sankt Valentinstag; Sie trugen ihn auf der Bahre bloss)
    Strauss Songs. Helen-Kay Eberley. EB-Sko ES 1005
    Strauss and Schumann. Edda Moser. Elec 1C 065-45 418
1409 **Du meines Herzens Krönelein,** op. 21/2
    Lieder Recital. Julia Hamari. Hung SLPX-12406
1410 **Einerlei,** op. 69/3
    Strauss Songs. Hilde Gueden. Lon 23212
1411 **Four Last Songs** (Frühling; September; Beim Schlafengehen; Im Abendrot)
    Strauss Songs Recital. Sylvia Sass. Hung SLPX-12397
    Strauss. Kiri Te Kanawa. Col M-35140
1412 **Freundliche Vision,** op. 48/1
    Song Recital. Montserrat Caballé. Ang SZB-3903
    Strauss Songs. Helen-Kay Eberley. Eb-Sko ES-1005
    Strauss Songs. Hilde Gueden. Lon 23212
1413 **Frühlingsfeier,** op. 56/5
    Strauss and Schumann. Edda Moser. Elec 1C 065-45 418
1414 **Frühlingsgedränge,** op. 26/1
    Strauss Lieder. Bernd Weikl. DG 2531 076
1415 **Für fünfzehn Pfennige,** op. 36/2
    German Lieder. Marilyn Horne. Lon OS-26302
    Strauss Lieder. Bernd Weikl. DG 2531 076
1416 **Geduld,** op. 10/5
    Strauss Lieder. Bernd Weikl. DG 2531 076
1417 **Hat gesagt—bleibt's nicht dabei,** op. 36/3
    German Romantic Songs. Elly Ameling. Phi 9500 350
1418 **Heimkehr,** op. 15/5
    Strauss and Wolf. Judith Blegen. RCA ARLI-1571
    Strauss Songs. Hilde Gueden. Lon 23212
    Schubert and Strauss. Leontyne Price. Ang SZ-37631
1419 **Heimliche Aufforderung,** op. 27/3
    Lieder Recital. Janet Baker. Odeon C 063 00391
    Song Recital. Montserrat Caballé. Ang SZB-3903
    Strauss Songs. Helen-Kay Eberley. Eb-Sko ES-1005
    Strauss Lieder. Bernd Weikl. DG 2531 076

1420 **Ich schwebe,** op. 48/2
    Strauss and Wolf. Judith Blegen. RCA ARLI-1571
    Song Recital. Montserrat Caballé. Ang SZB-3903
    Strauss Songs. Helen-Kay Eberley. Eb-Sko ES-1005
1421 **Ich trage meine Minne,** op. 31/2
    Song Recital. Montserrat Caballé. Ang SZB-3903
    Strauss Lieder. Bernd Weikl. DG 2531 076
1422 **Ich wollt ein Sträusslein binden,** op. 68/2
    Strauss and Wolf. Judith Blegen. RCA ARLI-1571
    Strauss Songs. Hilde Gueden. Lon 23212
1423 **Krämerspiegel,** op. 66 (Es war einmal ein Bock; Einst kam der Bock als
    Bote; Es liebte einst ein Hase; Drei Masken sag ich am Himmel stehn;
    Hast du ein Tongedicht vollbracht; O lieber Künstler sei ermahnt; Unser
    Feind; Von Händlern wird die Kunst bedroht; Es war einmal eine
    Wanze; Die Künstler sind die Schöpfer; Die Händler und die Macher;
    O Schröpferschwarm, O Händlerkreis)
    Strauss. Dietrich Fischer-Dieskau. Elec 1C 065-02 089
1424 **Liebeshymnus,** op. 32/3
    Lieder. Peter Anders. BWS IGI-382
    Concert. Janet Baker. Ang SQ-37199
1425 **Meinem Kinde,** op. 37/3
    Strauss Songs. Hilde Gueden. Lon 23212
    Strauss Songs Recital. Sylvia Sass. Hung SLPX-12397
1426 **Morgen,** op. 27/4
    Lieder Recital. Janet Baker. Odeon C 063 00391
    Schubert and Strauss. Leontyne Price. Ang SZ-37631
    Strauss. Kiri Te Kanawa. Col M-35140
    Strauss Lieder. Bernd Weikl. DG 2531 076
1427 **Mutterändelei,** op. 43/2
    Concert. Janet Baker. Ang SQ-37199
    Strauss. Kiri Te Kanawa. Col M-35140
1428 **Die Nacht,** op. 10/3
    Lieder Recital. Janet Baker. Odeon C 063 00391
    Song Recital. Montserrat Caballé. Ang SZB-3903
    Strauss Songs. Hilde Gueden. Lon 32312
    Strauss Lieder. Bernd Weikl. DG 2531 076
1429 **Nachtgang,** op. 29/3
    Strauss Lieder. Bernd Weikl. DG 2531 076
1430 **Nichts,** op. 10/2
    Strauss Songs. Helen-Kay Eberley. Eb-Sko ES-1005
    Strauss Lieder. Bernd Weikl. DG 2531 076
1431 **O süsser Mai,** op. 32/4
    Strauss Lieder. Bernd Weikl. DG 2531 076

STRAUSS, Richard—*continued*
1432 **Das Rosenband,** op. 36/1
    Concert. Janet Baker. Ang SQ-37199
    Strauss Song Recital. Sylvia Sass. Hung SLPX-12397
1433 **Ruhe, meine Seele,** op. 27/1
    Concert. Janet Baker. Ang SQ-37199
    Song Recital. Montserrat Caballé. Ang SZB-3903
    Strauss. Kiri Te Kanawa. Col M-35140
    Strauss Lieder. Bernd Weikl. DG 2531 076
1434 **Säusle, liebe Myrtle,** op. 68/3
1435 **Schlagende Herzen,** op. 29/2
    Strauss and Wolf. Judith Blegon. RCA ARLI-1571
    Strauss Songs. Hilde Gueden. Lon 23212
1436 **Schlechtes Wetter,** op. 69/5
    Song Recital. Montserrat Caballé. Ang SZB-3909
    Strauss Songs. Helen-Kay Eberley. Eb-Sko ES-1005
    Strauss Songs. Hilde Gueden. Lon 23212
    Strauss and Schumann. Edda Moser. Elec 1C 065-45 418
1437 **Schön sind, doch kalt,** op. 10/3
    German Lieder. Marilyn Horne. Lon OS-26302
1438 **Seitdem dein Aug',** op. 17/1
    Schubert and Strauss. Leontyne Price. Ang SZ-37631
1439 **Ständchen,** op. 17/2
    German Romantic Songs. Elly Ameling. Phi 9500 350
    Song Recital. Montserrat Caballé. Ang SZB-3903
    Strauss Songs. Helen-Kay Eberley. Eb-Sko ES-1005
    Strauss and Schumann. Edda Moser. Elec 1C 065-45 418
1440 **Der Stern,** op. 69/1
    Strauss and Wolf. Judith Blegen. RCA ARLI-1571
    Strauss Songs. Hilde Gueden. Lon 23212
1441 **Traum durch die Dämmerung,** op. 29/1
    German Romantic Songs. Elly Ameling. Phi 9500 350
    Song Recital. Montserrat Caballé. Ang SZB-3903
    Strauss Lieder. Bernd Weikl. DG 2531 076
1442 **Verführung,** op. 33/1
    Lieder. Peter Anders. BWS IGI-382
    Strauss Song Recital. Sylvia Sass. Hung SLPX-12397
1443 **Vier letzte Lieder.** *See* 1411
1444 **Waldseligkeit,** op. 49/1
    Lieder. Peter Anders. BWS IGI-382
    Song Recital. Montserrat Caballé. Ang SZB-3903
1445 **Wasserrose,** op. 22/4
    Schubert and Strauss. Leontyne Price. Ang SZ-37631

1446 Wer hat's getan
    Lieder der Jahrhundertwende. Dietrich Fischer-Dieskau. Odeon
    C 06502675
1447 Wiegenlied, op. 41/1
    Lieder Recital. Janet Baker. Odeon C 063 00391
    Song Recital. Montserrat Caballé. Ang SZB-3903
    Strauss Songs. Helen-Kay Eberley. Eb-Sko ES-1005
    Strauss. Kiri Te Kanawa. Col M-35140
1448 Wie sollten wir geheim sie halten, op. 19/4
    Song Recital. Montserrat Caballé. Ang SZB-3903
    Strauss Songs. Helen-Kay Eberley. Eb-Sko ES-1005
    Strauss Songs. Hilde Gueden. Lon 23212
    Lieder Recital. Julia Hamari. Hung SLPX-12406
    Strauss Lieder. Bernd Weikl. DG 2531 076
1449 Winterliebe, op. 48/5
    Lieder. Peter Anders. BWS IGI-382
1450 Winternacht, op. 15/2
    Strauss Lieder. Bernd Weikl. DG 2531 076
1451 Wozu noch Mädchen, op. 19/1
1452 Die Zeitlose, op. 10/7
    Strauss Songs. Helen-Kay Eberley. Eb-Sko-ES-1005
1453 Zueignung, op. 10/1
    Song Recital. Montserrat Caballé. Ang SZB-3903
    Strauss Song Recital. Sylvia Sass. Hung SLPX-12397
    Strauss. Kiri Te Kanawa. Col M-35140
    Strauss Lieder. Bernd Weikl. DG 2531 076

STRAVINSKY, Igor (1882-1971)
1454 Elegy for J. F. K.
    Lieder. Dorothy Dorow. Tele 642350 AW
1455 Pastorale
    Ein Liederabend. Elly Ameling. EMI 063-02375
1456 Three Songs from William Shakespeare (Musick To Heare; Full Fadom
Five Thy Father Lies; When Dasies Pied)
    Lieder. Dorothy Dorow. Tele 642350 AW

STREICHER, Theodor (1874-1940)
1457 Ist dir ein getreues, liebevolles Kind beschert
    Lieder der Neudeutschen. Dietrich Fischer-Dieskau. Odeon
    C 06502674

SZULC, Joseph (1875-1956)
1458 Clair de lune
Poems of Paul Verlaine. Carole Bogard. Cam CRS 2774

SZYMANOWSKI, Karol (1882-1937)
1459 **Four Songs,** op. 54 (Gentle Lady; Lean Out; Sleep Now; My Dove)
1460 **Pieśni Muezzina Szalonego** (Songs of the Lovesick Muezzin), op. 42
(Allah, Allah, Akbar Allah; O, ukochana ma; Ledwie blask słońca;
W południe miasto; O tej godzinie; Olio)
1461 **Rymy dziecięce** (Children's Rhymes), op. 49 (selections) (Kołysanka lalek;
Kołysanka gniadego konia)
1462 **Słopiewnie,** op. 46b (Słowisień; Zielone słowa; Św. Franciszek; Kalinowe
dwory; Wanda)
Songs of Szymanowski. Paulina Stark. Spectrum SR-160

TAILLEFERRE, Germaine (1892-1983)
1463 **Six Chansons françaises** (Non, la fidélité; Souvent un air de vérité; Mon
mari m'a diffamée; Hé! mon ami; Vrai Dieu, qui m'y confortera; On a dit
mal de mon ami)
Songs by Le Groupe des Six. Carole Bogard. Cam 2777
Songs of Les Six. Maria Lagios. Spectrum SR-147

TATE, Phyllis (b. 1911)
1464 **Apparitions** (The Wife of Usher's Well; The Suffolk Miracle; The Unquiet
Grave; Unfortunate Miss Bailey)
Hoddinott and Tate. Gerald English. Decca ZRG 691
1465 **Three Gaelic Ballads** (The Lake of Coolfin; Hark! The Soft Bugle; Hush
Song)
Hoddinott and Tate. Margaret Price. Decca ZRG 691

TCHAIKOVSKY, Piotr Ilyich (1840-93)
1466 **Again, as Before,** op. 73/6
Tchaikovsky Songs. Robert Tear. Argo ZRG 707
Russian Songs. Galina Vishnevskaya. EMI SLS 5055
1467 **As over Hot Embers,** op. 25/2
Tchaikovsky Songs. Robert Tear. Argo ZRG 707
1468 **Cradle Song,** op. 16/1
Tchaikovsky Songs. Robert Tear. Argo ZRG 707
Russian Songs. Galina Vishnevskaya. EMI SLS 5055
1469 **Disappointment,** op. 65/2

1470 **Don Juan's Serenade,** op. 38/1
Tchaikovsky Songs. Robert Tear. Argo ZRG 707
1471 **Do Not Believe Me, My Dear,** op. 6/1
Tchaikovsky Songs. Robert Tear. Argo ZRG 707
Russian Songs. Galina Vishnevskaya. EMI SLS 5055
1472 **Do Not Leave Me,** op. 27/23
Tchaikovsky Songs. Robert Tear. Argo ZRG 707
1473 **The Fearful Minute,** op. 28/6
Russian Songs. Galina Vishnevskaya. EMI SLS 5055
1474 **Great Deeds,** op. 60/11
Tchaikovsky Songs. Robert Tear. Argo ZRG 707
1475 **If I'd Only Known,** op. 47/1
Russian Songs. Galina Vishnevskaya. EMI SLS 5055
1476 **In the Clamour of the Ballroom,** op. 38/3
Tchaikovsky Songs. Robert Tear. Argo ZRG 707
Russian Songs. Galina Vishnevskaya. EMI SLS 5055
1477 **In This Moonlight,** op. 73/3
Russian Songs. Galina Vishnevskaya. EMI SLS 5055
1478 **Is It Not So?,** op. 16/5
Tchaikovsky Songs. Robert Tear. Argo ZRG 707
1479 **It Was in the Early Spring,** op. 38/2
Russian Songs. Galina Vishnevskaya. EMI SLS 5055
1480 **Mignon's Song,** op. 6/6
1481 **My Genius, My Angel, My Friend**
1482 **My Little Minx,** op. 27/6
1483 **O Stay!,** op. 16/2
1484 **Reconcilement,** op. 25/1
Tchaikovsky Songs. Robert Tear. Argo ZRG 707
1485 **Sleep, My Poor Friend,** op. 47/4
Russian Songs. Galina Vishnevskaya. EMI SLS 5055
1486 **They Kept Saying "You Fool,"** op. 25/6
1487 **Through the Window,** op. 60/10
1488 **To Forget So Soon**
Tchaikovsky Songs. Robert Tear. Argo ZRG 707
1489 **Was I Not a Little Blade of Grass?,** op. 47/7
1490 **Why?,** op. 6/5
Russian Songs. Galina Vishnevskaya. EMI SLS 5055

THOMAS, Ambroise (1811-96)
1491 **Le Soir**
Serate musicale. Joan Sutherland. Lon OSA-13132

THOMSON, Virgil (b. 1896)
1492 **Four Songs from William Blake** (The Divine Image; Tiger! Tiger!; The Land of Dreams; And Did Those Feet)
   Music of Virgil Thomson. Mack Harrell. CRI SRD 398
1493 **A Prayer to Saint Catherine**
   Von Stade Live. Frederica Von Stade. Col IM-37231

TIESSEN, Heinz (1887-1971)
1494 **Vöglein Schwermut**
   Lieder der Jahrhundertwende. Dietrich Fischer-Dieskau. Odeon
      C 06502675

TIPPETT, Michael (b. 1905)
1495 **Songs for Ariel** (Come unto These Yellow Sands; Full Fathom Five; Where the Bee Sucks)
   English Songs. Peter Pears. Argo ZK 28-29

TORRE, Francesco de la (ca. 1500)
1496 **Pámpano verde**
   Canciones españolas. Teresa Berganza. DG 2530 598

TOSTI, Paolo Francesco (1846-1916)
1497 **Luna d'estate**
   Luciano Pavarotti in Concert. Lon OS-26391
1498 **Malia**
   Luciano Pavarotti in Concert. Lon OS-26391
   Serenata. Renata Scotto. Col M-34501
1499 **Non t'amo più**
   Luciano Pavarotti in Concert. Lon OS-26391
1500 **La Serenata**
   Luciano Pavarotti in Concert. Lon OS-26391
   Serenata. Renata Scotto. Col M-34501

TURINA, Joaquin (1882-1949)
1501 **Anhelos**
   Seven Popular Spanish Songs. Montserrat Caballé. Lon OS 26575
1502 **Cantares**
   Canciones españolas. Teresa Berganza. DG 2530 598
   Seven Popular Spanish Songs. Montserrat Caballé. Lon OS 26575
   Recital of Songs and Arias. Renata Tebaldi. Lon R 23219

1503 **Canto a Sevilla** (Preludio; Semana Santa; Las fuentecitas del parque;
Noche de feria; El fantasma; La giralda; Ofrenda)
Song Recital. Montserrat Caballé. Ang SZB-3903
1504 **El Fantasma** (*Canto a Sevilla*). *See also* **1503**
Canciones españolas. Teresa Berganza. DG 2530 598
1505 **Farruca**
Seven Popular Spanish Songs. Montserrat Caballé. Lon OS 26575
1506 **Las locos por amor.** *See also* **1507**
Think on Me. Elly Ameling. CBS 36682
1507 **Poema en forma de canciones,** op. 19 (Dedicatoria; Nunca olvida;
Cantares; Los dos miedos. Las locas por amor)
A Recital of Spanish Songs. Jill Gomez. Saga 5409
1508 **Saeta**
Canciones españolas. Teresa Berganza. DG 2530 598
1509 **Si con mis deseos**
Seven Popular Spanish Songs. Montserrat Caballé. Lon OS 26575

VALVERDE, Joaquin (1846-1910)
1510 **Clavelitos**
Victoria de los Angeles in Concert. Ang SZ-37546

VAN DIEREN, Bernard (1884-1936)
1511 **Dream Pedlary**
1512 **Take, O Take Those Lips Away**
English Songs. Peter Pears. Argo ZK 28-29

VAUGHAN WILLIAMS, Ralph (1872-1958)
1513 **Along the Field** (We'll to the Woods No More; Along the Field; The Half-
Moon Westers Low; In the Morning; The Sigh that Heaves the Grasses;
Good-bye; Fancy's Knell; With Rue My Heart Is Laden)
Music for Voice and Violin. Catherine Malfitano. MHS 1976
1514 **As I Walked Out**
1515 **La Ballade de Jésus Christ**
1516 **The Brewer**
1517 **Bushes and Briars**
1518 **The Captain's Apprentice**
1519 **Chanson de Quête**
As I Walked Out. Robert Tear. Ang HQS 1412
1520 **A Clear Midnight**
English Songs. Ian Partridge. Peters PLE 136/7
1521 **The Cuckoo**
As I Walked Out. Robert Tear. Ang HQS 1412

VAUGHAN WILLIAMS, Ralph—*continued*
1522 **Four Nights**
    English Songs. Ian Partridge. Peters PLE 136/7
1523 **Geordie**
    As I Walked Out. Robert Tear. Ang HQS 1412
1524 **How Can the Tree but Wither?**
    English Songs. Ian Partridge. Peters PLE 136/7
1525 **How Cold the Wind Doth Blow** (with violin)
1526 **Joseph and Mary**
    As I Walked Out. Robert Tear. Ang HQS 1412
1527 **Joy, Shipmate, Joy!**
    English Songs. Ian Partridge. Peters PLE 136/7
1528 **The Lawyer** (with violin)
1529 **The Maiden's Lament**
1530 **The Morning Dew**
    As I Walked Out. Robert Tear. Ang HQS 1412
1531 **Motion and Stillness**
1532 **The New Ghost**
1533 **Nocturne**
    English Songs. Ian Partridge. Peters PLE 136/7
1534 **On Board a Ninety-Eight**
1535 **The Ploughman**
1536 **Reveillez-vous Piccarz**
    As I Walked Out. Robert Tear. Ang HQS 1412
1537 **The Roadside Fire** (*Songs of Travel*)
    Victoria de los Angeles in Concert. Ang SZ 37546
1538 **Rolling in the Dew**
1539 **The Saviour's Love**
1540 **Searching for Lambs** (with violin)
1541 **She's Like the Swallow**
    As I Walked Out. Robert Tear. Ang HWS 1412
1542 **Silent Noon**
    Think on Me. Elly Ameling. CBS 36682
1543 **Three Vocalises**
    The Ariel Ensemble. Julia Lovett. Orion 81411
1544 **The Truth Sent from Above**
    As I Walked Out. Robert Tear. Ang HQS 1412
1545 **The Twilight People**
1546 **The Water Mill**
    English Songs. Ian Partridge. Peters PLE 136/7

VERDI, Giuseppe (1813-1901)
1547 **Ad una stella**
    Verdi Songs. Klára Takács. Hung SLPX 12197

1548 **Brindisi**
> *Songs.* Renata Scotto. RCA V-AGLI 1-1341
> *Verdi Songs.* Klára Takács. Hung SLPX 12197

1549 **Deh, pietoso, oh addolorata**
1550 **Lésule**
1551 **In solitaria stanza**
1552 **Il mistero**
1553 **More, Elisa, lo stanco poeta**
1554 **Nell'orror di notte oscura**
1555 **Non t'accostare all'urna**
1556 **Perduta ho la pace**
> *Verdi Songs.* Klára Takács. Hung SLPX 12197

1557 **Il poveretto**
> *Serate musicali.* Joan Sutherland. Lon OSA 13132
> *Verdi Songs.* Klára Takács. Hung SLPX 12197

1558 **La seduzione**
> *Verdi Songs.* Klára Takács. Hung SLPX 12197

1559 **Lo spazzacamino**
> *Songs.* Renata Scotto. RCA V-AGLI 1-1341
> *Verdi Songs.* Klára Takács. Hung SLPX 12197

1560 **Stornello**
> *Songs.* Renata Scotto. RCA V-AGLI 1-1341
> *Verdi Songs.* Klára Takács. Hung SLPX 12197
> *Recital of Songs and Arias.* Renata Tebaldi. Lon 23219

1561 **Il tramonto**
1562 **La zingara**
> *Verdi Songs.* Klára Takács. Hung SLPX 12197

VIARDOT-GARCIA, Pauline (1821-1910)
1563 **Die Beschwörung**
1564 **Des Nachts**
1565 **Das Vöglein**
> *Lieder.* John Ostendorf. Leonarda LPI 107

VILLA-LOBOS, Heitor (1887-1959)
1566 **Suite for Voice and Violin** (The Young Girl and the Song; I Wish To Be Gay; The Peasant Girl of Brazil)
> *Music for Voice and Violin.* Catherine Malfitano. MHS 1976

VIVALDI, Antonio (1678-1741)
1567 **Agitata da due venti** (*Griselda*)
> *Arie antiche.* Montserrat Caballé. Lon OS 26618

VIVALDI, Antonio—*continued*
1568 Canto in prato, RV/R,623
   Vivaldi Motets. Elly Ameling. Phi 9500 556
1569 Un certo non so che (*L'Alteneide*)
   Italian Baroque Songs. Teresa Berganza. DG 2531 192
   Arie antiche. Montserrat Caballé. Lon OS 26618
1570 Chiare onde (*Ercole sui Termodonte*)
   Arie antiche. Montserrat Caballé. Lon OS 26618
1571 Col piacer della mia fede (*Arsilda, Regina di Ponto*)
   Recital. Cathryn Ballinger. Orion ORS 77280
1572 Da due venti (*Ercole sul Termodonte*)
   Arie antiche. Montserrat Caballé. Lon OS 26618
1573 Dille ch'il viver mio
   Songs of the Italian Baroque. Carlo Berganzi. HNH 4008
1574 Filli di gioa vuoi farmi morir
   Von Stade Live. Frederica Von Stade. Col IM-37231
1575 In furore, RV/R,626
1576 Nulla in mundo pax, RV/R,630
   Vivaldi Motets. Elly Ameling. Phi 9500 556
1577 O di tua man mi svena
   Songs of the Italian Baroque. Carlo Berganzi. HNH 4008
1578 O qui coeli, RV/R,631
   Vivaldi Motets. Elly Ameling. Phi 9500 556
1579 Piango, gemo, sospiro
   Italian Baroque Songs. Teresa Berganza. DG 2531 192
   Eighteenth Century Arias. Renata Tebaldi. Lon OS 26376
1580 Se cerca, se dice
   Songs of the Italian Baroque. Carlo Berganzi. HNH 4008
1581 Sposa, son disprezzata (*Bajazet*)
   Recital. Cathryn Ballinger. Orion ORS 77280
   Arie antiche. Montserrat Cabalé. Lon OS 26618
1582 Vieni, vieni, o mio diletto (*Ottone in Villa*)
   Arie antiche. Montserrat Caballé. Lon OS 22618

VIVES, Amadeo (b. 1871)
1583 El amor y los ojos
1584 Válgame Dios, que los ansares vuelan
1585 El retrato de Isabela
   Recital. Montserrat Caballé. Lon OS 26617

VUILLERMOZ, Jean (1906-40)
1586 Jardin d'amour
   Souvenirs. Elly Ameling. Col M 35119

WAGNER, Richard (1813-83)
1587 **Der Tannenbaum**
  Lieder der Neudeutschen. Dietrich Fischer-Dieskau. Odeon
    C 06502674
1588 **Träume** (*Wesendonck Lieder*). *See also* **1589**
  Think on Me. Elly Ameling. CBS 36682
  Farewell Recital. Lotte Lehmann. Pel LP 2009
1589 **Wesendonck Lieder** (Der Engel; Stehe still; Im Treibhaus; Schmerzen;
  Träume)
  Concert. Janet Baker. Ang SQ 37199

WALTON, William (1902-83)
1590 **Daphne**
  Song Recital. Kiri Te Kanawa. Col M 36667
1591 **Fain Would I Change That Note**
1592 **I Gave Her Cakes and I Gave Her Ale**
1593 **Lady, When I Behold the Roses**
1594 **My Love in Her Attire**
  Music for Voice and Guitar. Peter Pears. RCA V-AGLI-1281
1595 **Old Sir Faulk**
  Song Recital. Kiri Te Kanawa. Col M 36667
1596 **O Stay, Sweet Love**
  Music for Voice and Guitar. Peter Pears. RCA V-AGLI-1281
1597 **Through Gilded Trellises**
  Song Recital. Kiri Te Kanawa. Col M 36667
1598 **To Couple Is a Custom**
  Music for Voice and Guitar. Peter Pears. RCA V-AGLI-1281

WARD, Robert (b. 1917)
1599 **Ballad from "Pantaloon"**
  Anthology of American Music. William Parker. NW 300

WARLOCK, Peter (1894-1930)
1600 **After Two Years**
  English Songs. Ian Partridge. Peters PLE 136/7
1601 **Along the Stream**
  English Songs. Peter Pears. Argo ZK 28-29
1602 **As Ever I Saw**
  An Album of English Songs. Ian Partridge. MHS 4531
1603 **Away to Twiver**

WARLOCK, Peter—*continued*
1604 Balulalow
1605 The Frostbound Wood
1606 Jillian of Berry
1607 My Own Country
1608 Passing By
    English Songs. Ian Partridge. Peters PLE 136/7
1609 Piggesnie
    English Songs. Peter Pears. Argo ZK 28-29
1610 Pretty Ring Time
1611 Rest, Sweet Nymphs
1612 Sleep
1613 Sweet-and-Twenty
    English Songs. Ian Partridge. Peters PLE 136/7
1614 To the Memory of a Great Singer
    An Album of English Songs. Ian Partridge. MHS 4531
1615 Yarmouth Fair
    English Songs. Ian Partridge. Peters PLE 136/7
    An English Song Recital. Peter Pears. Eclipse ECS 545

WEBER, Carl Maria von (1786-1826)
1616 Abendsegen
    Weber Lieder. Hermann Prey. Elec 1C 065-30 782
1617 Der arme Minnesänger
1618 Betterlied
1619 Bach, Echo und Kuss
1620 Des Künstlers Abschied
1621 Einsam bin ich
    Weber Lieder. Peter Schreier. DG 2533 381
1622 Er an sie
1623 Es stürmt auf der Flur
1624 Die freien Sänger
1625 Die gefangenen Sänger
1626 Ich denke dein
    Weber Lieder. Hermann Prey. Elec 1C 065-30 782
1627 Ich sah ein Röschen am Wege stehn
    Weber Lieder. Hermann Prey. Elec 1C 065-30 782
    Weber Lieder. Peter Schreier. DG 2533 381
1628 Heitere Tage
1629 In euren Blicken
    Web er Lieder. Peter Schreier. DG 2533 381
1630 Klage
    Weber Lieder. Hermann Prey. Elec 1C 065-30 782

1631 Der kleine Fritz
1632 Ein König einst gefangen sass
1633 Lass mich schlummern
    Weber Lieder. Peter Schreier. DG 2533 381
1634 Liebe-Glühen
    Weber Lieder. Hermann Prey. Elec 1C 065-30 782
    Weber Lieder. Peter Schreier. DG 2533 381
1635 Liebeszauber
    Weber Lieder. Peter Schreier. DG 2533 381
1636 Meine Farben
1637 Meine Lieder, meine Sänge
1638 Mein Schatzerl ist hübsch
    Weber Lieder. Hermann Prey. Elec 1C 065-30 782
1639 Sanftes Licht
1640 Die Schäferstunde
    Weber Lieder. Peter Schreier. DG 2533 381
1641 Die Temperamente beim Verluste der Geliebten, op. 46 (Der
    Leichtmütige; Der Schwermütige; Der Liebemütige; Der Gleichmütige)
    Weber Lieder. Hermann Prey. Elec 1C 065-30 782
1642 Was zieht zu deinem Zauberkreise
    Weber Lieder. Hermann Prey. Elec 1C 065-30 782
    Weber Lieder. Peter Schreier. DG 2533 381
1643 Weh! Dass geschieden
    Weber Lieder. Peter Schreier. DG 2533 381
1644 Wenn ich ein Vöglein wär
    Weber Lieder. Hermann Prey. Elec 1C 065-30 782
1645 Wiegenlied
    Weber Lieder. Peter Schreier. DG 2533 381
1646 Wunsch und Entsagung
    Weber Lieder. Hermann Prey. Elec 1C 065-30 782
1647 Die Zeit
    Weber Lieder. Hermann Prey. Elec 1C 065-30 782
    Weber Lieder. Peter Schreier. DG 2533 381

WEBERN, Anton (1883-1945)
1648 Drei Lieder, op. 18 (Schatzerl klein, musst nit traurig; Erlösung;
    Ave Regina coelorum)
1649 Drei Volktexte, op. 17 (Armer Sünder, du; Liebste Jungfrau, wir sind
    dein; Heiland, unsre Missetaten)
    Lieder. Dorothy Dorow. Tele 6,42350 AW
1650 Erwachen aus dem tiefsten Traumesschosse
    Wirkung der neuen Wiener Schule im Lied. Dietrich Fischer-Dieskau.
    Odeon C 06502677

WEBERN, Anton—*continued*

1651 **Fünf geistliche Lieder,** op. 15 (Das Kreuz, das musst er tragen; Morgenlied; In Gottes Namen aufstehn; Mein Weg geht jetzt vorüber; Fahr hin, O Seel', zu deinem Gott)

1652 **Fünf Kanons nach lateinischen Texten,** op. 16 (Christus factus est; Dormi Jesu, mater ridet; Crux fidelis inter omnes; Asperges me; Crucem tuam adoramus, Domine)
  Lieder. Dorothy Dorow. Tele 6,42350 AW

1653 **Kunftag I**

1654 **Das lockere Saatgefilde lechzet krank**
  Wirkung der neuen Wiener Schule im Lied. Dietrich Fischer-Dieskau. Odeon C 06502677

1655 **Sechs Lieder nach Gedichten von Georg Trakl,** op. 14 (Die Sonne; Abendlied I, II, III; Nachts; Gesang einer gefangenen Amsel)
  Lieder. Dorothy Dorow. Tele 6,42350 AW

1656 **Trauer I** (Maximin)
  Wirkung der neuen Wiener Schule im Lied. Dietrich Fischer-Dieskau. Odeon C 06502677

WECKERLIN, Jean Baptiste (1821-1910)

1657 **Bergerettes** (Aminte [Tambourin]; Bergère légère; Chaque chose a son temps; Je connais un berger discret; Jeunes fillettes; Maman, dites-moi; Menuet d'Exaudet; La Mère bontemps; Non, je ne crois pas; Non, je n'irai plus au bois; O ma tendre Musette; Philis, plus avare que tendre; Que ne suis-je la fougère; Venez, agréable printemps)

1658 **Pastourelles** (Ah, mon berger; La Batelière; Les Belles Manières; Chassant dans nos forêts; Lison dormait; Menuet tendre; Paris est au roi; Ronde villageoise)
  Bergerettes et Pastourelles. Mady Mesplé. Pathé 2C 069-14044

1659 **Tambourin.** *See also* **1657**
  Think on Me. Elly Ameling. CBS 36682

WEIGL, Karl (1881-1949)

1660 **Beatrix**
  Karl Weigl Songs. George Shirley. Orion ORS 81407

1661 **Blaue Nacht**

1662 **Es goss mein volles Leben**
  Karl Weigl Songs. Betty Allen. Orion ORS 81407

1663 **Five Lieder aus "Phantasus"** (Aus weissen Wolken baut sich ein Schloss; Dann losch das Licht; Über die Welt hin ziehen die Wolken; In meinem schwarzen Taxuswald; Auf einem vergoldeten Blumenschiff)
  Karl Weigl Songs. Judith Raskin. Orion ORS 81407

1664 **Halleluja der Sonne**
   Karl Weigl Songs. William Warfield. Orion ORS 81407
1665 **Liebeslied**
1666 **Lied der Schiffermädels**
   Karl Weigl Songs. Betty Allen. Orion ORS 81407
1667 **O Nacht, du silberbleiche**
   Karl Weigl Songs. William Warfield. Orion ORS 81407
1668 **Schlummerlied**
   Karl Weigl Songs. George Shirley. Orion ORS 81407
1669 **Schmied Schmerz**
   Karl Weigl Songs. William Warfield. Orion ORS 81407
1670 **Seele**
   Karl Weigl Songs. George Shirley. Orion ORS 81407
1671 **Spielmannslied**
   Karl Weigl Songs. Betty Allen Orion ORS 81407
1672 **Das unsichtbare Licht**
   Karl Weigl Songs. George Shirley. Orion ORS 81407
1673 **Wiegenlied**
   Karl Weigl Songs. William Warfield. Orion ORS 81407

WEILL, Kurt (1900-50)
1674 **Frauentanz,** op. 10 (Wir haben die winterlange Nacht; Wo zwei
   Herzenliebe; Ach wär' mein Lieb; Dieser Stern im Dunkeln; Eines Maien-
   morgens schön; Ich will Trauern lassen stehn; Ich schlaf, ich wach)
   Song Cycles for Soprano Plus. Edith Gordon Ainsberg. Leonarda
   LPI 106

WEINGARTNER, Felix Paul (1863-1942)
1675 **Liebesfeier**
   Lieder der Neudeutschen. Dietrich Fischer-Dieskau. Odeon
   C 06502674

WEISGALL, Hugo (b. 1912)
1676 **End of Summer** (After Lunch; Hearing Someone Sing a Poem by Yüan
   Chen; De Senectute)
   American Contemporary-Vocal Music. Charles Bressler. CRI SD-343
1677 **Four Songs on Poems by Adelaide Crapsey,** op. 1 (Old Love; Song; Oh,
   Lady, Let the Sad Tears Fall; Dirge)
   American Songs. Carolyn Heafner. CRI SD 462
1678 **The Golden Peacock** (Undzer Rebenyu; Lomir zikh befrayen; Mayn Harts
   veyne in mir; Baleboste Zisinke; Schlof mayn Kind; Der rebbe Elimeylekh;
   Di goldene Pave)

WEISGALL, Hugo—*continued*
1679 **Translations** (Knoxville, Tennessee; Song; Child Song; Poem; Poem [second version]; Poem [Celia Dropkin]; The Rebel; A City by the Sea) *Song Cycles by Hugo Weisgall.* Judith Raskin. CRI SD 417

WERNICK, Richard (b. 1934)
1680 **Haiku of Basho**
1681 **Moonsongs from the Japanese**
American Contemporary Voices and Instruments. Neva Pilgrim. CRI SD 379
1682 **Songs of Remembrance**
Davies and Wernick. Jan De Gaetani. None H-71342

WETZEL, Justus Hermann (1879-1973)
1683 **An meine Mutter**
1684 **Der Kehraus**
Lieder der Jahrhundertwende. Dietrich Fischer-Dieskau. Odeon C 06502675

WILSON, Olly (b. 1937)
1685 **Sometimes**
Other Voices. William Brown. CRS SD 370

WILSON, Richard (b. 1941)
1686 **The Ballad of Longwood Glen**
Wilson, Thome and Yannay. Paul Sperry. CRI S-437

WOLF, Hugo (1860-1903)
1687 **Hugo Wolf Lieder,** volume 1
Mörike Lieder (selections)
Abschied; An den Schlaf; An die Geliebte; An eine Aeolsharfe; Auf ein altes Bild; Auf eine Christblume; Auf einer Wanderung; Auftrag; Begegnung; Bei einer Trauung; Denk'es, O Seele; Er ist's; Der Feuerreiter; Frage und Antwort; Fussreise; Der Gärtner; Gebet; Die Geister am Mummelsee; Der Genesene an die Hoffnung; Gesang Weylas; Heimweh; Im Frühling; In der Frühe; Der Jäger; Jägerlied; Karwoche; Der Knabe und das Immlein; Der König bei der Krönung; Lebewohl; Lied eines Verliebten; Lied vom Winde; Neue Liebe; Nimmersatte Liebe; Peregrina I, II; Schlafendes Jesuskind; Selbstgeständnis; Seufzer; Storchen-botschaft; Der Tambour; Um Mitternacht; Verborgenheit; Wo find ich Trost?; Zitronenfalter im April; Zum neuen Jahr; Zur Warnung) *Dietrich Fischer-Dieskau.* DG 2709 053

1688 Hugo Wolf Lieder, volume II

Goethe Lieder (excerpts)

Anakreons Grab; Beherzigung I, II; Blumengruss; Cophtisches Lied I, II; Dank des Paria; Dies zu deuten bin erbötig; Epiphanias; Erschaffen und beleben; Frech und froh I, II; Frühling übers Jahr; Ganymed; Genialisch Treiben; Gleich und gleich; Grenzen der Menschheit; Gutmann und Gutweib; Harfenspieler Lieder I, II, III; Hätt ich irgend wohl Bedenken; Komm, Liebchen, komm; Königlich Gebet; Locken, haltet mich gelangen; Der neue Amadis; Nicht Gelegenheit macht Diebe; Ob der Koran von Ewigkeit sei; Phänomen; Prometheus; Der Rattenfänger; Ritter Kurts Braufahrt; Der Sänger; Sankt Nepomuks Vorabend; Der Schäfer; So lang man nüchtern ist; Spottlied; Trunken müssen wir alle sein; Wanderers Nachtlied; Was in der Schenke waren heute; Wenn ich dein gedenke; Wie wollt ich heiter bleiben

Selected Songs

Abendbilder; Du bist wie eine Blume; Frage nicht; Herbst; Herbstentschluss; Mädchen mit dem roten Mündchen; Mit schwarzen Segeln; Wenn ich in deine Augen seh'; Wie des Mondes Abbild zittert; Wo wird einst

Dietrich Fischer-Dieskau. DG 2709 066

1689 Hugo Wolf Lieder, volume III

Eichendorff Lieder

Andenken; Auf der Wanderung; Ein Grab; Erwartung; Der Freund; Der Glücksritter; Heimweh; In der Fremde I, II, IV; Ja, die Schönst! Ich sagt' es offen; Knabentod; Lieber alles; Liebesfrühling; Liebesglück; Der Musikant; Nach dem Abschiede; Nachruf; Die Nacht; Nachtzauber; Rückkehr; Der Scholar; Der Schreckenberger; Der Schwalben Heimkehr; Seemanns Abschied; Der Soldat I, II; Ständchen; Das Ständchen; Über Nacht; Unfall; Verschiegene Liebe; Der verzweifelte Liebhaber

Drei Gedichte von Michelangelo

Wohl denk ich oft; Alles endet, was entstehet; Fühlt meine Seele das ersehnte Licht von Gott

Selected Songs

Biterolf; Frohe Botschaft; Frühlingsglocken; Gesellenlied; Keine Gleicht von allen Schönen; Liebchen, wo bist du?; Liebesbotschaft; Lied des transferierten Zettel; Morgenstimmung; Skolie; Sonne der Schlummerlosen; Ständchen (Reinick); Nachtgruss; Wächterlied auf der Wartburg; Wohin mit der Freud'?; Zur Ruh', zur Ruh'

Dietrich Fischer-Dieskau. DG 2709 067

WOLF, Hugo—*continued*
1690 **Ach, des Knaben Augen** (*Spanisches Liederbuch*)
   Lieder Recital. Janet Baker. Odeon C 063-00391
   Strauss and Wolf. Judith Blegen. RCA ARLI 1571
1691 **Anakreons Grab** (Goethe)
   Lieder. Elisabeth Schwarzkopf. BWS IGI-382
1692 **Andenken** (Matthisson)
1693 **Auch kleine Dinge** (*Italienisches Liederbuch*). *See also* **1711**
   Wolf Lieder. Solveig Faranger. BIS LP-161
1694 **Auf ein altes Bild** (Mörike)
   To My Friends. Elisabeth Schwarzkopf. Lon OS 26592
1695 **Auf einer Wanderung** (Mörike)
   German Lieder. Marilyn Horne. Lon OS 26302
1696 **Bedeckt mich mit Blumen** (*Spanisches Liederbuch*)
   Lieder. Elisabeth Schwarzkopf. BWS IGI-382
1697 **Bei einer Trauung** (Mörike)
   To My Friends. Elisabeth Schwarzkopf. Lon OS 26592
1698 **Die Bekehrte** (Goethe)
   Strauss and Wolf. Judith Blegen. RCA ARLI-1571
1699 **Blumengruss** (Goethe)
   Song Recital. Kire Te Kanawa. Col M 36667
1700 **Die ihr schwebet** (*Spanisches Liederbuch*)
   Lieder Recital. Janet Baker. Odeon C 063-00391
   Strauss and Wolf. Judith Blegen. RCA ARLI-1571
1701 **Elfenlied** (Mörike)
   To My Friends. Elisabeth Schwarzkopf. Lon OS 26592
1702 **Epiphanias** (Goethe)
   Strauss and Wolf. Judith Blegen. RCA ARLI-1571
1703 **Fussreise** (Mörike)
   To My Friends. Elisabeth Schwarzkopf. Lon OS 26592
1704 **Der Gärtner** (Mörike)
   German Romantic Songs. Elly Ameling. Phi 9500 350
1705 **Geh, Geliebter, geh jetzt** (*Spanisches Liederbuch*)
   Wolf Lieder. Solveig Faranger. BIS LP-161
1706 **Der Genesene an die Hoffnung** (Mörike)
   German Lieder. Marilyn Horne. Lon OS-26302
1707 **Heimweh** (Eichendorff)
   To My Friends. Elisabeth Schwarzkopf. Lon OS 26592
1708 **Herr, was trägt der Boden hier?** (*Spanisches Liederbuch*)
   Lieder Recital. Janet Baker. Odeon C 063-00391
1709 **Im Frühling** (Mörike)
   Lieder. Elisabeth Schwarzkopf. BWS IGI-382
1710 **In dem Schatten meiner Locken** (*Spanisches Liederbuch*)
   Wolf Lieder. Solveig Faranger. BIS LP-161

1711 Italienisches Liederbuch (Auch kleine Dinge; Mir ward gesagt; Ihr seid die die Allerschönste; Gesegnet sei; Selig ihr Blinden; Wer rief dich denn; Der Mond hat eine schwere Klag' erhoben; Nun lass uns Frieden schliessen; Dass doch gemalt all' deine Reize wären; Du denkst mit einem Fädchen; Wie lange schon was immer mein Verlangen; Nein, junger Herr; Hoffärtig seid Ihr, schönes Kind; Geselle, woll'n wir uns in Kutten hüllen; Mein Liebster ist so klein; Ihr jungen Leute; Und willst du deinen Liebsten sterben sehen; Heb' auf dein blondes Haupt; Wir haben beide; Mein Liebster singt am Haus; Man sagt mir, deine Mutter woll' es nicht; Ein Ständchen Euch zu bringen; Was für ein Lied soll dir gesungen werden; Ich esse nun mein Brot nicht trocken mehr; Mein Liebster hat zu Tische mich geladen; Ich liess mir sagen; Schon streckt' ich aus im Bett; Du sagst mir, dass ich keine Fürsten sei; Wohl kenn; ich Euren Stand; Lass sie nur gehn; Wie soll ich frölich sein; Wass soll der Zorn; Sterb' ich, so hüllt in Blumen meine Glieder; Und steht Ihr am Morgen auf; Benedeit die sel'ge Mutter; Wenn du, mein Liebster, steigst zum Himmel auf; Wie viele Zeit verlor ich; Wenn du mich mit den Augen streifst; Gesegnet sei das Grün; O wär' dein Haus durchsichtig wie ein Glas; Heut' Nacht erhob ich mich, um Mitternacht; Nicht länger kann ich singen; Schweig' einmal still; O wüsset du; Verschling' der Angrund; Ich hab' in Penna einen Liebsten wohnen)
Elly Ameling and Tom Krause. None NB-78014
Christa Ludwig and Dietrich Fischer-Dieskau. DG 2707 114

1712 Italienisches Liederbuch (excerpts) (Auch kleine Dinge; Mir ward gesagt; Wer rief dich denn; Du denkst mit einem Fädchen; Wie lange schon; Ihr jungen Leute; Mein Liebster singt; Schweig' einmal still; Ich hab in Penna).
See also **1711**
German Songs. Benita Valente. Desmar DSM 1010

1713 Jägerlied (Mörike)
To My Friends. Elisabeth Schwarzkopf. Lon OS 26592

1714 Die Kleine (Mörike)
Wolf Lieder. Solveig Faringer. BIS LP-161

1715 Lebe wohl (Mörike)
To My Friends. Elisabeth Schwarzkopf. Lon OS 26592

1716 Mausfallen-Sprüchlein (Mörike)
Wolf Lieder. Solveig Faringer. BIS LP-161
To My Friends. Elisabeth Schwarzkopf. Lon OS 26592

1717 Mein Liebster (Heyse)

1718 Mignon (Goethe)
German Lieder. Marilyn Horne. Lon OS 26302

1719 Mir ward gesagt (*Italienisches Liederbuch*). *See also* **1711**
Wolf Lieder. Solveig Faringer. BIS LP-161

WOLF, Hugo—*continued*
1720 **Mögen alle bösen Zungen** (*Spanisches Liederbuch*)
   Wolf Lieder. Solveig Faringer. BIS LP-161
   Lieder. Elisabeth Schwarzkopf. BWS IGI-382
1721 **Mörike Lieder** (excerpts) (Abschied; An die Geliebte; Auf einer
   Wanderung; Begegnung; Bei einer Trauung; Der Feuerreiter; Fussreise;
   Der Genesene an die Hoffnung; Im Frühling; In der Frühe; Der Jäger;
   Jägerlied; Lebewohl; Neue Liebe; Peregrina I, II; Storchenbotschaft;
   Verborgenheit)
   Mörike Lieder. Dietrich Fischer-Dieskau. DG 2530 584
1722 **Nein junger Herr** (*Italienisches Liederbuch*). *See also* **1711**
   Wolf Lieder. Solveig Faringer. BIS LP-161
1723 **Nimmersatte Liebe** (Mörike)
1724 **Nixe Binsefuss** (Mörike)
   To My Friends. Elisabeth Schwarzkopf. Lon OS 26592
1725 **Nun lass uns Frieden** (*Italienisches Liederbuch*). *See also* **1711**
   Wolf Lieder. Solveig Faringer. BIS LP-161
1726 **Nun wandre Maria** (*Spanisches Liederbuch*)
   Lieder Recital. Janet Baker. Odeon C 063-00391
   Strauss and Wolf. Judith Blegen. RCA ARLI-1571
1727 **O wär' dein Haus** (*Italienisches Liederbuch*). *See also* **1711**
1728 **Sagt seid Ihr es, feiner Herr** (*Spanisches Liederbuch*)
   Wolf Lieder. Solveig Faringer. BIS LP-161
1729 **Schlafendes Jesuskind** (Mörike)
   Strauss and Wolf. Judith Blegen. RCA ARLI-1571
1730 **Selbstgeständnis** (Mörike)
   To My Friends. Elisabeth Schwarzkopf. Lon OS 26592
1731 **Die Spröde** (Goethe)
   Strauss and Wolf. Judith Blegen. RCA ARLI-1571
   Wolf Lieder. Solveig Faringer. BIS LP-161
1732 **Storchenbotschaft** (Mörike)
   To My Friends. Elisabeth Schwarzkopf. Lon OS 26592
1733 **Ein Stündlein wohl vor Tag** (Mörike)
   Wolf Lieder. Solveig Faringer. BIS LP-161
1734 **Und willst du deinen Liebsten** (*Italienisches Liederbuch*). *See also* **1711**
   Recital. Elena Gerhardt. Disc KG-G-4
1735 **Das verlassene Mägdlein** (Mörike)
   Wolf Lieder. Solveig Faringer. BIS LP-161
   To My Friends. Elisabeth Schwarzkopf. Lon OS 26592
1736 **Verschwiegene Liebe** (Eichendorff)
1737 **Waldmädchen** (Eichendorff)
   Strauss and Wolf. Judith Blegen. RCA ARLI-1571
1738 **Wer rief dich denn?** (*Italienisches Liederbuch*). *See also* **1711**

1739 **Wiegenlied** (Mörike)
   Wolf Lieder. Solveig Faringer. BIS LP-161
1740 **Wiegenlied im Sommer** (Reinick)
   German Romantic Songs. Elly Ameling. Phi 9500 350
1741 **Wie lange schon** (*Italienisches Liederbuch*). *See also* **1711**
   Wolf Lieder. Solveig Faringer. BIS LP-161
1742 **Die Zigeunerin** (Eichendorff)
   Lieder. Elisabeth Schwarzkopf. BWS IGI-382
1743 **Zum neuen Jahr** (Mörike)
   Strauss and Wolf. Judith Blegen. RCA ARLI-1571

WOLF-FERRARI, Ermanno (1876-1948)
1744 **Il campiello**
   Serenata. Renata Scotto. Col M 34501

YANNAY, Yehuda (b. 1937)
1745 **At the End of the Parade**
   Wilson, Thome and Yannay. Lawrence Weller. CRI S 437

ZAIMONT, Judith Lang (b. 1945)
1746 **Two Songs for Soprano and Harp** (At Dusk in Summer; The Ruined Maid)
   Song Cycles for Soprano Plus. Berenice Bramson. Leonarda LPI 106

ZELLER, Karl (1842-98)
1747 **Sei nicht bös** (Der Oversteiger)
1748 **Wie mein Ahn'l zwanzig Jahr** (Der Vogelhändler)
   The Art of Elisabeth Schumann. Sera 60320

SECTION *2 Record Companies*

Record Companies

Works of One Composer

BACH, Johann Sebastian
Angel S-37229. *Bach Arias*

Ach, bleibe doch (Cantata 11); Bereite dich, Zion (Christmas Oratorio); Bist du bei mir (Notebook of Anna Magdalena Bach); Es ist vollbracht (St. John Passion); Et exultavit (Magnificat in D Major); Gelobet sei der Herr (Cantata 129); Hochgelobter Gottessohn (Cantata 6); Komm, du süsse Todesstunde (Cantata 161); Lobe, Zion, deinen Gott (Cantata 190); Saget, saget mir geschwinde (Easter Oratorio); Wohl euch ihr auserwählten Seelen (Cantata 34)

> Janet Baker, m-sop; Academy of St. Martin-in-the-Fields, Neville Marriner

BEETHOVEN, Ludwig van
Metronome MPS 158,004. *Beethoven Lieder*

An Laura; Das Blümchen Wunderhold; Elegie auf den Tod eines Pudels; Feuerfarb; Klage; Lied; Das Liedchen von der Ruhe; Mailied; Marmotte; Selbstgespräch; Urians Reise um die Welt. Piano: Dressler Variations

> Max van Egmond, bar; Wilhelm Krumbach, pf, hpschd; Männerchorgruppe

BEETHOVEN, Ludwig van—*continued*
RCA ARL1-3417. *Scottish English, Irish and Welsh Songs*
The British Light Dragoons; Cease Your Funning; Come Draw We Round the Cheerful Ring; Cupid's Kindness; Good Night; The Kiss, Dear Maid, Thy Lip Has Left; O Harp of Erin; O Mary, at Thy Window Be; On the Massacre of Glencoe; The Pulse of an Irishman; The Return to Ulster; Sally in Our Alley; The Soldier; 'Tis Sunshine at Last; The Vale of Clywd; When Mortals All to Rest Retire
> Robert White, ten; Yo-Yo Ma, vlc; Ani Kavafian, vln; Samuel Sanders, pf

BOULANGER, Lili
Spectrum UNI-PRO SR-126. *Boulanger*
Clairières dans le ciel
> Paulina Stark, sop; David Garvey, pf

BRAHMS, Johannes
Angel S-37519. *Brahms Lieder*
Auf dem Kirchhofe; Geistliches Wiegenlied; Gestille Sehnsucht; Der Jäger; Regenlied; Sapphische Ode; Ständchen; Therese; Vergebliches Ständchen; Vier ernste Gesänge; Wie Melodien zieht es mir
> Janet Baker, m-sop; Andre Previn, pf

Columbia M-34535. *An Evening of Brahms Songs*
Feldeinsamkeit; Immer leiser wird mein Schlummer; Liebestreu; Mädchenlied; Die Mainacht; Ruhe, süssliebchen, im Schatten; Sapphische Ode; Ständchen; Der Tod, das ist die kühle Nacht; Von ewiger Liebe; Zigeunerlieder
> Christa Ludwig, m-sop; Leonard Bernstein, pf

Philips 9500 398. *Brahms Lieder*
Agnes; Botschaft; Dein blaues Augen; Des Liebsten Schwur; Der Frühling; Heimweh; Immer leiser wird mein Schlummer; In den Beeren; Der Jäger; Komm bald; Das Mädchen spricht; Sandmännchen; Spanisches Lied; Die Trauernde; Vergebliches Ständchen; Von ewiger Liebe; Von waldbekränzter Höhe; Wiegenlied
> Elly Ameling, sop; Dalton Baldwin, pf

Philips 9500 785. *Brahms Lieder*
Botschaft; Geistliches Wiegenlied; Gestille Sehnsucht; Immer leiser wird mein Schlummer; Die Mainacht; Meine Liebe ist grün; O komme, holde Sommernacht; Ständchen; Therese; Der Tod, das ist die kühle Nacht; Von ewiger Liebe; Wie Melodien zieht es mir
> Jessye Norman, sop; Geoffrey Parsons, pf; Ulrich von Wrochem, vla

BRITTEN, Benjamin
London STS-15166. *Britten*
A Charm of Lullabies; Folk Songs: The Ash Grove; The Bonny Earl of Moray; Come You Not from Newcastle; O Can Ye Sew Cushions?; Oliver Cromwell; The Salley Gardens; Sweet Polly Oliver; There's None to Soothe; The Trees They Grow So High; O Waly, Waly
Bernadette Greevy, sop; Paul Hamburger, pf
London SR 33257. *Benjamin Britten*
A Birthday Hansel; Canticle V—The Death of Saint Narcissus; Ca' the Yowes; O Can Ye Sew Cushions; Second Lute Song from *Gloriana;* Suite for Harp, op. 83
Peter Pears, ten; Osian Ellis, hp

CARISSIMI, Giacomo
Oiseau-Lyre DSLO 547. *Carissimi Cantatas*
Amor mio, che cosa è questo?; Apritevi, Inferni; Bel tempo per me se n'andò; Deh, memoria; In un mar di pensieri; No, no mio core; Suonerà l'ultima tromba; V'intendo, v'intendo occhi
Martyn Hill, ten; Robert Spencer, lute; Trevor Jones, vla da gamba; Christopher Hogwood, hpschd, org

CHOPIN, Frederic
Everest 3370. *Chopin Songs*
Seventeen Polish Songs; Two Posthumous Songs
Annette Celine, sop; Felicja Blumenthal, pf
Helois H-88001. *Chopin*
Seventeen Polish Songs
Eugenia Zareska, m-sop; Giorgio Favaretto, pf

CLÉRAMBAULT, Louis Nicolas
Archive 2533 442. *Clérambault*
Médee; Orphée
Rachel Yakar, sop; Reinhard Goebel, vln; Wilbert Hazelzet, fl; Charles Medlam, vla da gamba; Alan Curtis, hpschd

DALLAPICCOLA, Luigi
1750 Archive 1782. *The Music of Luigi Dallapiccola*
Cinque canti; Divertimento in quattro esercizi; Quattro liriche di Antonio Machado; Rencesvals
Anna Carol Dudley, sop; Tom Buckner, ten; Marvin Tartak, pf; Ensemble, Hughes

DUKE, John
  Cambridge CRS 2776. *Songs by John Duke*
  Five Songs on Texts by Sara Teasdale; Four Chinese Love Lyrics; Four
  Poems by e. e. cummings; Four Poems by Emily Dickinson; Six Poems
  by Emily Dickinson; Stopping by Woods on a Snowy Evening
  Carole Bogard, sop; John Duke, pf

DUPARC, Henri
  EMI C 169-16387. *Duparc Mélodies*
  Au pays où se fait la guerre; Chanson triste; Elégie; Extase; Le Galop;
  L'Invitation au voyage; Lamento; Le Manoir de Rosemonde; Phidylé;
  Sérénade Florentine; Soupir; Testament; La Vague et la cloche; La Vie
  antérieure
  Jane Rhodes, m-sop; Christian Icaldi, pf.

FAURÉ, Gabriel
  Connoisseur Society CS-2127/8. *Fauré*
  Complete Songs
  Elly Ameling, sop; Gérard Souzay, bar; Dalton Baldwin, pf
  Musical Heritage Society 3438/3448. *Fauré*
  Complete Songs
  Jacques Herbillon, bar; Anne-Marie Rodde, sop; Sonia Nigoghossian,
  sop; Theodore Paraskivesco, pf

GRIEG, Edvard
  London R 23220. *Grieg Songs*
  Den Aergjerrige; En Drom; Eros; Det forste mode; Fra Monte Pincio; Der
  Gynger en Bad pa Bolge; Hytten; Jeg elsker Dig; Jeg giver mit digt til
  varen; I Liden hojt deroppe; Liden Kirsten; Med en Primula veris; Med en
  Vandlijie; Millom Rosor
  Kirsten Flagstad, sop; Edwin McArthur, pf

HANDEL, George Frideric
  Deutsche Grammophon 2536 360. *Handel*
  Neuen deutsche Arien
  Catarina Ligendza, sop; Chamber Ensemble
  Philips 6670 113. *Handel*
  Crudel tiranno amor (cantata); Piangerò la sorte mia; Silete venti (motet)
  Elly Ameling, sop; English Chamber Orch., Leppard

Telefunken 642367 AW. *Italian Solo Cantatas*
Un'alma innamorata; Armida abbondonata; Figlio d'alte speranze; Nel dolce dell'oblio
Marjanne Kweksilber, sop; Musica Antiqua, Koopman

HAYDN, Franz Joseph
Philips 6769 064. *Joseph Haydn Lieder*
Abschiedslied; Als einst mit Weibes Schönheit; An Iris; An Thyrsis; Auch die sprödeste der Schönen; Auf meine Vaters Grab; Bald wehen uns des Frühlings Lüfte; Beim Schmerz; Content; Cupid; Despair; Der erste Kuss; Fidelity; Gegenliebe; Geistliches Lied; Der Gleichsinn; Gott, erhalte Franz den Kaiser; Jeder meint, der Gegenstand; Lachet nicht, Mädchen; The Lady's Looking-Glass; Die Landlust; Das Leben ist ein Traum; Liebeslied; Lob der Faulheit; The Mermaid's Song; Minna; O fliess, ja wallend fliess in Zähern; O liebes Mädchen, höre mich; O Tuneful Voice; A Pastoral Song; Pensi a me sì fido amante; Piercing Eyes; Pleasing Pain; Recollection; Sailor's Song; Der schlaue und dienstfertige Pudel; Eine sehr gewöhnliche Geschichte; She Never Told Her Love; The Spirit's Song; Das strickende Mädchen; Sympathy; Un tetto umil; Trachten will ich nicht auf Erden; Trost unglücklicher Liebe; Der Verlassene; The Wanderer; Zufriedenheit; Die zu späte Ankunft der Mutter
Elly Ameling, sop; Jörg Demus, pf

IVES, Charles
Deutsche Grammophon 2530 6976. *Ives Songs*
Abide with Me; Ann Street; At the River; Autumn; The Children's Hour; A Christmas Carol; Disclosure; Elegie; A Farewell to Land; Feldeinsamkeit; From "The Swimmers"; Ich grolle nicht; In Flanders Fields; Tom Sails Away; Two Little Flowers; Weil' auf mir; West London; Where the Eagle; The White Gulls
Dietrich Fischer-Dieskau, bar; Michael Ponti, pf
Nonesuch H 71325. *Ives Songs*
Ann Street; At the River; The Cage; A Christmas Carol; The Circus Band; A Farewell to Land; From "Paracelsus"; The Housatonic at Stockbridge; The Indians; The Innate; In the Mornin'; Like a Sick Eagle; Majority; Memories; Serenity; The Things Our Fathers Loved; Thoreau
Jan De Gaetani, m-sop; Gilbert Kalish, pf

LISZT, Franz
Deutsche Grammophon 2740 254. *Liszt Lieder*
Anfangs wollt ich fast verzagen; Blume und Dufte; Comment, disaient-ils;

LISZT, Franz—*continued*
Der du von dem Himmel bist; Des Tages laute Stimmen schweigen; Drei
Lieder aus Schillers "Wilhelm Tell"; Die drei Zigeuner; Du bist wie eine
Blume; Enfant, si j'étais roi; Englein hold im Lockengold; Es muss ein
wunderbares sein; Es rauschen die Winde; Ein Fichtenbaum steht
einsam; Gastbelza; Gestorben war ich; Hohe Liebe; Ich möchte hingehn;
Ihr Glocken von Marling; Im Rhein, im schönen Strome; In Liebeslust;
J'ai perdu ma force et ma vie; Kling leise, mein Lied; Lasst mich ruhen;
Die Loreley; Morgens steh' ich auf und frage; Oh, quand je dors; O Lieb,
so lang du lieben kannst; Schwebe, schwebe blaues Auge; S'il est un
charmant gazon; Die stille Wasserrose; La Tombe et la rose; Der traurige
Mönch; Tre sonetti di Petrarca; Über allen Gipfeln ist Ruh'; Die Vätergruft;
Vergiftet sind meine Lieder; Le Vieux Vagabond; Wer nie sein Brot mit
Tränen ass; Wieder möcht' ich dir begegnen; Wie singt die Lerche schön
 Dietrich Fischer-Dieskau, bar; Daniel Barenboim, pf

LOEWE, Karl
 Claves D 8106. *Loewe*
Gregor auf dem Stein; Kaiser Karl V (Vier historische Balladen)
 Roland Hermann, bar; Geoffrey Parsons, pf

MENDELSSOHN, Felix
 Deutsche Grammophon 2530 596. *On Wings of Song*
Altdeutsches Frühlingslied; And'res Maienlied; Auf Flügeln des Gesanges;
Bei der Wiege; Erster Verlust; Frage; Frühlingslied (op. 19a/1, op. 34/3,
op. 47/3); Gruss; Hirtenlied; Im Herbst; Jägdlied; Minnelied; Der Mond;
Neue Liebe; Pagenlied; Reiselied; Schilflied; Venetianisches Gondellied;
Wanderlied; Winterlied
 Peter Schreier, ten; Walter Olbertz, pf
 EMI SLS 805. *Mendelssohn Lieder*
Allnächtlich im Traume; Altdeutsches Lied; Altes Kirchenlied; An die
Entferne; And'res Maienlied; Auf der Wanderschaft; Auf Flügeln des
Gesanges; Bei der Wiege; Der Blumenkranz; Da lieg' ich unter den
Bäumen; Das erste Veilchen; Erster Verlust; Es lauschte das Laub;
Frühlingslied (op. 19a/1, op. 34/3, op. 47/3); Der Mond; Morgengruss;
Nachtlied; Neue Liebe; O Jugend, o schöne Rosenzeit; Pagenlied;
Reiselied (op. 19a/6, op. 34/6); Scheidend; Schilflied; Schlafloser
Augen Leuchts; Tröstung; Venetianisches Gondellied; Volkslied; Das
Waldschloss; Wanderlied; Warnung vor dem Rhein; Wenn sich zwei
Herzen scheiden; Winterlied
 Dietrich Fischer-Dieskau, bar; Wolfgang Sawallisch, pf

MEYERBEER, Giacomo
Deutsche Grammophon 2533 295. *Meyerbeer Lieder*
    Cantique du Trappiste; Le Chant du dimanche; Der Garten des Herzens;
    Hör ich das Liedchen klingen; Komm; Menschenfeindlich; Mina; Le Poète
    mourant; Die Rose, die Lilie, die Taube; Die Rosenblätter; Scirocco;
    Sicilienne; Sie und ich; Ständchen
        Dietrich Fischer-Dieskau, bar; Karl Engel, pf

MOZART, Wolfgang Amadeus
London OS 26661. *Mozart Concert Arias*
    Ah, lo previdi . . . Ah, t'invola; Chi sa, chi sa, qual sia; Nehmt meinen
    Dank, ihr holden Gönner; Non temer, amato bene; Oh, temerario Arbace
    . . . Per quel paterno amplesso; Resta, oh cara; Vado, ma dove?
        Kiri Te Kanawa, sop; Rainer Küchl, vln; Vienna Chamber Orch.,
        Fisher
London OS 26662. *Mozart Concert Arias*
    Ah, non lasciarmi, no; Alma grande e nobil core; Misera, dove son . . .
    Ah, non son io che parlo; Un moto di gioia; Per pietà, bell'idol mio;
    Schon lacht der holde Frühling; Se tutti i mali miei; Voi avete un
    cor fidele
        Edita Gruberova, sop; Vienna Chamber Orch., Fischer
Philips 6747 483. *Mozart Lieder*
    Abendempfindung; Als aus Ägypten; Als Luise die Briefe; Die Alte; An
    Chloe; An die Freude; An die Freundschaft; Die betrogene Welt; Dans un
    bois solitaire; Des kleinen Friedrichs Geburtstag; Der Frühling; Geheime
    Liebe; Die gross mütige Gelassenheit; Ich würd' auf meinen Pfad; Das
    Kinderspiel; Die kleine Spinnerin; Komm, liebe Zither, komm; Lied beim
    Auszug in das Feld; Lied der Freiheit; Das Lied der Trennung; Lied zur
    Gesellenreise; Meine Wünsche; Un moto do gioia; O Gotteslamm; Oiseaux,
    si tous les ans; Ridente la calme; Sehnsucht nach dem Frühlinge; Sei du
    mein trost; Das Traumbild; Das Veilchen; Verdankt sei es dem Glanz
    der Grossen; Die Verschweigung; Warnung; Wie unglücklich bin ich nit;
    Der Zauberer; Die Zufriedenheit; Die Zufriedenheit in niedrigen Stande
        Elly Ameling, sop; Dalton Baldwin, pf
Vanguard VSD-71246. *Mozart Lieder*
    Abendempfindung; An Chloe; Die betrogne Welt; Des kleinen Friedrichs
    Geburtstag; Der Frühling; Ich würd' aif, meinem Pfad; Das Kinderspiel;
    Komm, liebe Zither, komm; Lied der Freiheit; Das Lied der Trennung;
    Sehnsucht nach dem Frühling; Sei du mein Trost; Das Traumbild; Das
    Veilchen; Wie unglücklich bin ich nit; Die Zufriedenheit
        Peter Schreier, ten; Jörg Demus, pf

PARRY, Hubert
Argo ZK 44. *Parry: English Lyrics*
And Yet I Love Her till I Die; Blow, Blow Thou Winter Wind; Bright Star;
From a City Window; Looking Backward; Love Is a Bable; O Mistress
Mine; Marian; No Longer Mourn for Me; On a Time the Amorous Silvy;
Take, O Take Those Lips Away; There; There Be None of Beauty's
Daughters; Thine Eyes Still Shine for Me; Weep You No More; A Welsh
Lullaby; When Comes My Gwen; When Icicles Hang by the Wall; When
Lovers Meet Again; When We Two Parted
Robert Tear, ten; Philip Ledger, pf

PERLE, George
CRI SD 403. *Songs by George Perle*
Thirteen Dickinson Songs; Two Rilke Songs
Bethany Beardslee, sop; Morey Ritt, pf; George Perle, pf

PURCELL, Henry
Enigma K 53569. *Sweeter than Roses; Purcell Songs*
Ah! How Sweet It Is To Love; Bonvica's Song; Crown the Altar; The
Earth Trembled; An Evening Hymn; I Attempt from Love's Sickness to
Fly; If Music Be the Food of Love; I'll Sail upon the Dog-Star; I See She
Flies Me Ev'rywhere; Let the Night Perish; Lord, What Is Man, Lost Man;
A Morning Hymn; Music for a While; A Roundelay; Since from My Dear
Astrea's Sight; Sweeter than Roses; Take Not a Woman's Anger
III. Harpsichord: A New Ground
Ian Partridge, ten; George Malcolm, hpschd
Harmonia Mundi HM-249. *Purcell Songs*
An Evening Hymn; Fairest Isle; From Rosy Bow'rs; I Attempt from
Love's Sickness to Fly; If Music Be the Food of Love; Music for a While;
Not All My Torments; O Lead Me to Some Peaceful Gloom; The Plaint;
Retired from Any Mortal's Sight; Since from My Dear Astrea's Sight;
Sweeter than Roses; Thrice Happy Lovers
Alfred Deller, ct; Wieland Kuijken, bs viol; William Christie, hpschd;
Roderick Skeaping, bar viol

RACHMANINOFF, Sergei
London OS 26428
Rachmaninoff Songs, volume I
Elisabeth Söderström, sop; Vladimir Ashkenazy, pf
London OS 26453
Rachmaninoff Songs, volume II
Elisabeth Söderström, sop; Vladimir Ashkenazy, pf

London OS-26433
Rachmaninoff Songs, volume III
Elisabeth Söderström, sop; Vladimir Ashkenazy, pf
London OS-26559
Rachmaninoff Songs, volume IV
Elisabeth Söderström, sop; Vladimir Ashkenazy, pf
London OS-26615
Rachmaninoff Songs, volume V
Elizabeth Söderström, sop; Vladimir Ashkenazy, pf
Orion ORS-75180. *Rachmaninoff Songs*
All Love You So; A-oo; At Night in My Garden; Child! Like a Flower;
Daisies; Dream; Floods of Spring; He Took It All Away from Me; Love
Has Lost Its Joy; Night Is Sad; The Rat Catcher; Time; To Her; To the
Children; Water Lily
Peter Del Grande, bar; Vladimir Pleshakov, pf

ROCHBERG, George
CRI SD 360. *Rochberg*
Songs in Praise of Krishna
Neva Pilgrim, sop; George Rochberg, pf

ROREM, Ned
Desto DC 7147. *Ned Rorem*
Ariel. Chorus: Gloria
Phyllis Curtin, sop; Helen Vanni, m-sop; Joseph Rabbai, cl;
Ned Rorem, pf

ROSSI, Luigi
Harmonia Mundi 1010. *Cantate*
Erminia sventurata; Gelosia; Lamento della regina de svezia; Lamento de
Zaida Mora; Mentro sorge dal mar; Quando spiega la notte; Sopra conca
d'argento
Judith Nelson, sop; Wieland Kuijken, bas di viole; William Christie,
hpschd, positive organ

SATIE, Erik
Arabesque 8053-L. *Erik Satie*
Le Chapelier; Daphénéo; La Diva de l'Empire; Trois Autres Mélodies;
Trois Mélodies; Geneviève de Brabant; Mass for the Poor
Mady Mesplé, sop; Aldo Ciccolini, pf; Gaston Litaize, org; Orch.,
Paris, Dervaux; Chor. of René Duclos, Laforge

SATIE, Erik—*continued*
Unicorn RHS 338. *An Erik Satie Entertainment*
 Songs: Les Anges La Diva de l'Empire; Elégie; Hymne: Salut Drapeau;
 Je te veux; Sylvie; Tendrement; Trois Autres Mélodies; Two Arias from
 "Geneviève de Brabant." Piano: Gnossienne no. 2; Gymnopédie no. 1;
 Je te veux; Pièces froides, no. 2; Le Piccadilly; Poudre d'or; Vexations
 Meriel Dickinson, m-sop; Peter Dickinson, pf

SCHOENBERG, Arnold
RCA ARLI-1231. *Schoenberg*
 Brettl-Lieder; Nine Early Songs
 Marni Nixon, sop; Leonard Stein; pf

SCHUBERT, Franz
Arabesque 8107/3L. *Schubert Song Recital*
 Abschied; Am Meer; An die Musik; Der Doppelgänger; Erlkönig; Das
 Fischermädchen; Liebeslauchen; Lied eines Schiffers an die Dioskuren;
 Der Musensohn; Die schöne Müllerin; Ständchen, D. 889, D. 957;
 Die Taubenpost; Der Wanderer; Wer nie sein Brot mit Tränen ass; Wer
 sich der Einsamkeit ergibt; Widerschein; Die Winterreise
 Gerhard Hüsch, ten; Hanns Udo Müller, pf; Gerald Moore, pf
Bruno Walter Society IGI-386. *Schubert Lieder Recital*
 Abschied; Alinde; An den Tod; An die Musik; Atys; Des Sängers Habe;
 Geheimes; Griesengesang; Harfenspieler I, III; Der Kreuzzug; Die liebe
 hat gelogen; Liedesend; Meeres Stille; Orest und Tauris; Orpheus;
 Pilgerweise; Der Schäfer und der Reiter; Schiffers Scheidelied; Tiefes
 Lied; Totengräbers Heimweh; Der Wanderer; Wanderers Nachtlied;
 Das Zügenglöcklein
 Hans Hotter, bs-bt; Michael Raucheisen, pf
Deutsche Grammophon 2530 528. *Schubert Lieder*
 An den Mond; Bertha's Lied in der Nacht; Dass sie hier gewesen; Klärchens
 Lied; Lied der Anna Lyle; Lied der Mignon I, II; Lilla an die Morgenröte;
 Das Mädchen; Mignons Gesang; Sehnsucht; Ständchen; Wehmut; Der Zwerg
 Christa Ludwig, con; Irwin Gage, pf
Deutsche Grammophon 2530 544
 Die schöne Müllerin
 Dietrich Fischer-Dieskau, bar; Gerald Moore, pf
Deutsche Grammophon 2530 988. *Schubert Lieder*
 Abendbilder; Am Fenster; Auf der Bruck; Auf der Donau; Aus "Heliopolis";
 Des Sängers Habe; Fischerweise; Im Frühling; Liebeslauschen; Der Schiffer;
 Die Sterne; Der Strom; Totengräbers Heimweh; Der Wanderer; Wehmut;
 Das Zügenglöcklein
 Dietrich Fischer-Dieskau, bar; Sviatoslav Richter, pf

Deutsche Grammophon 2531 325. *Schubert*
Schwanengesang
Hermann Prey, bar; Leonard Hokanson, pf
Deutsche Grammophon 3301 237. *Schubert*
Die Winterreise
Dietrich Fischer-Dieskau, bar; Daniel Barenboim, pf
Enigma VAR 1019. *Schubert Lieder*
An die Laute; An die Musik; An Silvia; Auflösung; Bei dir allein; Dass
sie hier gewesen; Der Einsame; Fischerweise; Die Forelle; Ganymed;
Liebesbotschaft; Der Schiffer; Ständchen; Die Sterne; Über Wildemann;
Der Wanderer an den Mond; Wanderers Nachtlied
Ian Partridge, ten; Jennifer Partridge, pf
Harmonia Mundi HM-1023/4. *Schubertiade*
Abendstern; Auf dem Strom; Auflösung; Ave Maria; Dass sie hier
gewesen; Die Forelle; Frühlingsglaube; Heidenröslein; Der Hirt auf dem
Felsen; Im Frühling; Jäger, ruhe von der Jagd; Lachen und Weinen;
Liebesbotschaft; Lob der Tränen; Nachtviolen; Raste, Krieger; Seligkeit;
Suleika; Suleikas zweiter Gesang. Piano: Valse in B; Galopp in G;
Dances Allemandes; Impromptu in G♭; Moment Musical in A♭
Judith Nelson, sop; Jörg Demus, pf; Alfred Prinz, cl; Franz
Söllner, horn
Peters PLE 123. *Schubert*
Auf dem Strom; Four Songs on Italian Texts; Gott im Frühlinge; Herbst;
Der Hirt auf dem Felsen; Die Sommernacht; Der Winterabend
Elly Ameling, sop; Irwin Gage, pf; Guy Deplus, cl; Julia
Studebaker, horn
Philips 6500 704. *Schubert Lieder*
An die Laute; An Silvia; Der Blumenbrief; Du liebst mich nicht; Der
Einsame; Im Abendrot; Die Liebe hat gelogen; Der liebliche Stern; Das
Mädchen; Die Männer sind méchant; Minnelied; Nacht and Träume;
Romance aus Rosamunde; Schlummerlied; Seligkeit; Die Sterne
Elly Ameling, sop; Dalton Baldwin, pf
Philips 9500 169. *Schubert Songs*
Ave Maria; Faust—Scene I; Gretchen am Spinnrade; Gretchens Bitte;
Jäger, ruhe von der Jagd; Die junge Nonne; Der König in Thule; Raste,
Krieger; Suleika; Suleikas zweiter Gesang
Elly Ameling, sop; Dalton Baldwin, pf

SCHUMAN, William
CRI SD 439. *William Schuman*
In Sweet Music; Time to the Old; The Young Dead Soldiers
Rosalind Rees, sop; Orpheus Trio; Thomas Muraco, pf; Robin
Graham, Fr. hn; White Mts. Fest. Orch., Schwarz

SCHUMANN, Robert
Angel S-37043. *Schumann*
    Frauenliebe und Leben; Liederkreis, op. 39
       Elisabeth Schwarzkopf, sop; Geoffrey Parsons, pf
Angel S-37222. *Schumann*
    Frauenliebe und Leben; Liederkreis, op. 39
       Janet Baker, m-sop; Daniel Barenboim, pf
Deutsche Grammophon 2530 543. *Schumann Lieder*
    Liederkreis, op. 24; Myrthen (excerpts)
       Dietrich Fischer-Dieskau, bar; Christoph Eschenbach, pf
Deutsche Grammophon 2531 290. *Schumann*
    Dichterliebe; Liederkreis, op. 39
       Dietrich Fischer-Dieskau, bar; Christoph Eschenbach, pf
Deutsche Grammophon 2531 323. *Schumann*
    Frauenliebe und Leben; Die Blume der Ergebung; Frühlingslust; Hinaus
    ins Freie; Kinderwacht; Die letzten Blumen; Liebeslied; Lied der Suleika;
    Mond, meiner Seele Liebling; Reich mir die Hand; Der Sandmann;
    Schmetterling; Singet nicht in Trauertönen; Weit! Weit!
       Edith Mathis, sop; Christoph Eschenbach, pf
Deutsche Grammophon 2709 074
    Schumann Lieder, volume I
       Dietrich Fischer-Dieskau, bar; Christoph Eschenbach, pf
Deutsche Grammophon 2709 079
    Schumann Lieder, volume II
       Dietrich Fischer-Dieskau, bar; Christoph Eschenbach, pf
Deutsche Grammophon 2709 088
    Schumann Lieder, volume III
       Dietrich Fischer-Dieskau, bar; Christoph Eschenbach, pf
Eurodisc 201 298 366. *Robert Schumann*
    Frauenliebe und Leben; Er ist's; Erstes Grün; Frühlingsgruss;
    Frühlingslust; Mein Garten; Mignon; Mit Myrten und Rosen; Reich
    mir die Hand; Röselein, Röselein; Schneeglöckchen
       Lucia Popp, sop; Geoffrey Parsons, pf
Odeon C 06302184. *Lieder von Robert Schumann*
    Abendlied; Aufträge; Geisternähe; Herzeleid; Der Himmel hat eine Träne
    geweint; Jasminenstrauch; Die Kartenlegerin; Liebeslied; Lied der Suleika;
    Loreley; Die Lotusblume; Melancholie; Mignon; Der Nussbaum; Philine;
    Resignation; Die Soldatenbraut; Stiller Vorwurf; Volksliedchen; Widmung
       Elly Ameling, sop; Jörg Demus, pf
Philips 6769 037. *Schumann*
    Liederalbum für die Jugend; Liederkreis, op. 39
       Elly Ameling, sop; Jörg Demus, pf

Philips 9500 110. *Schumann*
Frauenliebe und Leben; Liederkreis, op. 39
Jessye Norman, sop; Irwin Gage, pf
RCA RL 25126. *Schumann Lieder*
An den Mond; Der arme Peter; Aufträge; Aus den östlichen Rosen;
Freisinn; Frühlingsfahrt; Fünf Lieder; Geisternähe; Geständnis; Der
Hidalgo; Jasminenstrauch; Der Knabe mit dem Wunderhorn; Leis' rudern
hier; Loreley; Mädchen-Schwermut; Marienwürmchen; Meine Töne still
und heiter; Mein schöner Stern; Nur ein lächender Blick; O, wie lieblich
ist das Mädchen; Romanze; Der Page; Requiem; Sechs Gedichte;
Sehnsucht; Setze mir nicht; Sitz' ich allein; So sei gegrüsst viel
tausendmal; Ständchen; Talismane; Wanderers Nachtlied; Weh, wie
zornig ist das Mädchen; Wenn durch die Piazetta; Widmung;
Zigeunerliedchen; Zum Schloss
　　Peter Schreier, ten; Norman Shetler, pf
Rococo 53762. *Schumann*
Dichterliebe; Kerner Lieder
　　Gérard Souzay, bar; Alfred Cortot, pf; Dalton Baldwin, pf

SPIES, Claudio
CRI SD 445. *Music by Claudio Spies*
Three Songs on Poems by May Swenson; Five Sonnet-Settings; Animula
Vugula; Blandula; Bagatelle; 4 Davidas
　　Christine Whittlesey, sop; Johana Arnold, alto; Davis Ronis, ten;
　　Jan Opalach, bs; Henry Martin, pf; Alan Feinberg, pf; Claudio
　　Spies, cond

STRAUSS, Richard
Deutsche Grammophon 2531 076. *Strauss Lieder*
Ach Lieb, ich muss nun scheiden; Ach weh mir unglückhaftem Mann;
Breit über mein Haupt; Cäcilie; Frühlingsgedränge; Für fünfzehn Pfennige;
Geduld; Heimliche Aufforderung; Ich trage meine Minne; Morgen; Die
Nacht; Nachtgang; Nichts; O süsser Mai; Ruhe, meine Seele; Traum
durch die Dämmerung; Wie sollten wir geheim sie halten; Winternacht;
Zueignung
　　Bernd Weikl, bar; Cord Garben, pf
Eb-Sko ES 1005. *Strauss Songs*
Am Ufer; Befreit; Breit' über mein Haupt; Drei Lieder der Ophelia aus
"Hamlet"; Freundliche Vision; Heimliche Aufforderung; Ich schwebe;
Nichts; Schlechtes Wetter; Ständchen; Wiegenlied; Wie sollten wir
geheim sie halten; Wozu noch Mädchen; Die Zeitlose
　　Helen-Kay Eberley, sop; Donald Isaak, pf

STRAUSS, Richard—*continued*
Electrola 1C 065-02 089. *Richard Strauss*
Krämerspiegel
Dietrich Fischer-Dieskau, bar; Gerald Moore, pf
Hungaroton SLPX-12397. *Strauss Song Recital*
Cäcilie; Four Last Songs; Meinem Kinde; Das Rosenband; Verführung;
Zueignung
Sylvia Sass, sop; Hungarian State Orch., Lukacs
London 23212. *Strauss*
Als mir dein Lied erklang; Befreit; Einerlei; Freundliche Vision; Heimkehr;
Ich wollt ein Sträusslein binden; Meinem Kinde; Die Nacht; Säusle, liebe
Myrtle; Schlagende Herzen; Schlechtes Wetter; Der Stern; Wie sollten
wir geheim sie halten
Hilde Gueden, sop; Friedrich Gulda, pf
London M-35140. *Strauss*
Four Last Songs; Befreit; Morgen; Mutterändelei; Ruhe, meine Seele;
Wiegenlied; Zueignung
Kiri Te Kanawa, sop; London Sym., Andrew Davis

SZYMANOWSKI, Karol
Spectrum SR-160. *Songs of Szymanowski*
Four Songs; Pieśni Muezzina Szalonego; Rymy dziecięce (selections);
Słopiewnie
Paulina Stark, sop; David Garvey, pf

TCHAIKOVSKY, Piotr Ilyich
Argo ZRG 707. *Tchaikovsky Songs*
Again, as Before; As over Hot Embers; Cradle Song; Disappointment;
Don Juan's Serenade; Do Not Believe Me, My Dear; Do Not Leave Me;
Great Deeds; In the Clamour of the Ballroom; Is It Not So?; Mignon's
Song; My Genius, My Angel, My Friend; My Little Minx; O Stay!;
Reconcilement; They Kept Saying "You Fool"; Through the Window;
To Forget So Soon
Robert Tear, ten; Philip Ledger, pf

THOMSON, Virgil
CRI SRD 398. *Music of Virgil Thomson*
Four Songs from William Blake; Three Portraits; Three Pictures for
Orchestra
Mack Harrell, bar; Philadelphia Orch., Ormandy, Thomson

VAUGHAN WILLIAMS, Ralph
Angel HQS 1412. *As I Walked Out*
  As I Walked Out; La Ballade de Jésus Christ; The Brewer; Bushes and
  Briars; The Captain's Apprentice; Chanson de Quête; The Cuckoo;
  Geordie; How Cold the Wind Doth Blow; Joseph and Mary; The Lawyer;
  The Maiden's Lament; The Morning Dew; On Board a Ninety-Eight;
  The Ploughman; Reveillez-vous Piccarz; Rolling in the Dew; The
  Saviour's Love; Searching for Lambs; She's Like the Swallow; The
  Truth Sent from Above
    Robert Tear, ten; Philip Ledger, pf; Hugh Bean, vla

VERDI, Giuseppe
Hungaroton SLPX 12197. *Verdi Songs*
  Ad una stella; Brindisi; Deh, pietoso, oh addolorata; L'esule; In solitaria
  stanza; Il mistero; More, Elisa, lo stanco poeta; Nell'orror di notte
  oscura; Non t'accostare all'urna; Perduta ho la pace; Il poveretto;
  La desuzione; Lo Spazzacamino; Stornello; Il tramonto; La zingara
    Klára Takács, m-sop; Sándor Falvai, pf

VIVALDI, Antonio
Philips 9500 556. *Vivaldi Motets*
  Canto in prato; In furore; Nulla in mundo pax; O qui coeli
    Elly Ameling, sop; Jeffrey Tate, hpschd; English chamber Orch.,
    Vittorio Negri

WEBER, Carl Maria von
Deutsche Grammaphon 2533 381. *Weber Lieder*
  Der arme Minnesänger; Bach, Echo und Kuss; Betterlied; Des Künstlers
  Abschied; Einsam bin ich; Heitere Tage; Ich sah ein Röschen am Wege
  stehn; In euren Blicken; Der kleine Fritz; Ein König einst gefangen sass;
  Lass mich schlummern; Liebe-Glühen; Liebeszauber; Sanftes Licht; Die
  Schäferstunde; Was zieht zu deinem Zauberkreise; Weh! Dass
  geschieden; Wiegenlied; Die Zeit
    Peter Schreier, ten; Konrad Ragossnig, pf
Electrola 1C 065-30 782. *Weber Lieder*
  Abendsegen; Er an sie; Es stürmt auf der Flur; Die freien Sänger; Die
  gefangenen Sänger; Ich denke dein; Ich sah ein Röschen am Wege
  stehn; Klage; Liebe-Glühen; Meine Farben; Meine Lieder, meine Sänge;
  Mein Schatzerl ist hübsch; Die Temperamente beim Verluste der
  Geliebten; Was zieht zu deinem Zauberkreise; Wenn ich ein Vöglein
  wär; Wunsch und Entsagung; Die Zeit
    Hermann Prey, bar; Leonard Hokanson, pf

WEIGL, Karl
Orion ORS 81407. *Karl Weigl Songs*
Abenstunde (duet); Beatrix; Blaue Nacht; Ehestand der Freude (duet);
Es goss mein volles Leben; Five Lieder aus "Phantasus"; Halleluja der
Sonne; Hymn (duet); In goldenen Fülle (duet); Liebeslied; Lied der
Schiffermädels; O Nacht, du silberbleiche; Schlummerlied; Schmied
Schmerz; Seele; Spielmannslied; Das unsichtbare Licht; Der Wanderer
und das Blumenmädchen (duet); Wiegenlied
    Betty Allen, m-sop; Colette Boky, sop; Judith Raskin, sop; George
    Shirley, ten; William Warfield, bar; David Garvey, pf

WEISGALL, Hugo
CRI SD 417. *Song Cycles by Hugo Weisgall*
The Golden Peacock; Translations
    Judith Raskin, sop; Morey Ritt, pf

WOLF, Hugo
BIS LP-161. *Wolf Lieder*
Andenken; Auch kleine Dinge; Geh, Geliebter, geh jetzt; In dem Schatten
meiner Locken; Die Kleine; Mausfallen-Sprüchlein; Mir ward gesagt; Mögen
alle bösen Zungen; Nein junger Herr; Nun lass uns Frieden; O wär' dein
Haus; Sagt seid Ihr es, feiner Herr; Die Spröde; Ein Stündlein wohl vor Tag;
Das verlassene Mägdlein; Wer rief dich denn?; Wiegenlied; Wie lange schon
    Solveig Faranger, sop; Thomas Schuback, pf
Deutsche Grammophon 2530 584. *Mörike Lieder*
Mörike Lieder (excerpts)
    Dietrich Fischer-Dieskau, bar; Sviatoslav Richter, pf
Deutsche Grammophon 2707 114. *Wolf*
Italienisches Liederbuch
    Christa Ludwig, m-sop; Dietrich Fischer-Dieskau, bar; Daniel
    Barenboim, pf
Deutsche Grammophon 2709 053
Hugo Wolf Lieder, volume I
    Dietrich Fischer-Dieskau, bar; Daniel Barenboim, pf
Deutsche Grammophon 1709 066
Hugo Wolf Lieder, volume II
    Dietrich Fischer-Dieskau, bar; Daniel Barenboim, pf
Deutsche Grammophon 2709 067
Hugo Wolf Lieder, volume III
    Dietrich Fischer, bar; Daniel Barenboim, pf
Nonesuch NB-78014. *Wolf*
Italienisches Liederbuch
    Elly Ameling, sop; Tom Krause, bar; Irwin Gage, pf

Works of Two or More Composers, by Record Company

ANGEL

SZB-3903. *Song Recital*
MONTSALVATGE: Cinco ciones negras
STRAUSS: Als mir dein Lied erklang; Des Dichters Abendgang;
Freundliche Vision; Heimliche Aufforderung; Ich schwebe; Ich trage
meine Minne; Die Nacht; Ruhe, meine Seele; Schlechtes Wetter;
Ständchen; Traum durch die Dämmerung; Waldseligkeit; Wiegenlied;
Wie sollten wir geheim sie halten; Zueignung
TURINA: Canto a Sevilla
    Montserrat Caballe, sop; Alexis Weissenberg, pf
S-37172. *Scottish Folk Songs*
BEETHOVEN: Bonny Laddie; Cease Your Funning; Faithfu' Johnnie;
Highland Laddie; The Sweetest Lad Was Jamie
HAYDN: The Birks of Abergeldie; The Brisk Young Lad; Cumbernauld
House; Duncan Gray; Green Grow the Rushes; I'm O'er Young to
Marry Yet; John Anderson; Love Will Find Out the Way; My Ain Kind
Dearie; My Boy Tammy; O Bonny Lass; O Can Ye Sew Cushions?; The
Ploughman; Shepherds, I Have Lost My Love; Sleepy Bodie; Up in the
Morning Early; The White Cockade
    Janet Baker, m-sop; Yehudi Menuhin, vln; George Malcomb, hpschd
SQ-37199. *Concert*
BRAHMS: Alto Rhapsody
STRAUSS: Liebeshymnus; Mutterändelei; Der Rosenband; Ruhe, meine
Seele
WAGNER: Wesendonck Lieder
    Janet Baker, m-sop; London Phil., Boult; John Alldis Choir
S-37401. *Chausson and Duparc*
CHAUSSON: Poème de l'amour et de la mer
DUPARC: Au pays où se fait la guerre; L'Invitation au voyage; Le Manoir
de Rosemonde; Phidylé; La Vie antérieure
    Janet Baker, m-sop; Lonson Sym. Orch., Previn
SZ-37546. *De los Angeles in Concert*
BRAHMS: Liebestreu; Vergebliches Ständchen
FALLA: Jota; Polo
HANDEL: Vanne, sorella ingrata
MONTEVERDI: Maledetto sia l'aspetto; Ohimè! Ch'io cado ohimè!
MONTSALVATGE: Punto de Habenera
NIN: Asturiana; Piano musciano
RODRIGO: Canción del Grumete; De los álamos vengo, madre;
Trovadoresca
SCHUBERT: Lachen und Weinen; Mein

ANGEL—*continued*
SCHUBERT: Lachen und Weinen; Mein
VALVERDE: Clavelitos
VAUGHAN WILLIAMS: The Roadside Fire
BARRERA Y CALLEJA: Adiós Granada
TRADITIONAL: I Will Walk with My Love; Blow the Wind Southerly
    Victoria de los Angeles, sop; Gerald Moore, pf

SZ-37631. *Schubert and Strauss Lieder*
SCHUBERT: Die Allmacht; Ave Maria; Gretchen am Spinnrade; Die junge
    Nonne; Liebesbotschaft; Mignons Lied II; Nacht und Träume
STRAUSS: Als mir dein Lied erklang; Befreit; Breit' über mein Haupt;
    Cäcilie; Heimkehr; Morgen; Seitdem dein Aug'; Wasserrose
    Leontyne Price, sop; David Garvey, pf

1750 Archive Records S-1766. *An Album of French Songs*
BRITTEN: French Folk Song Arrangements: La Noël passée; Le Roi s'en
    va-t'en chasse; Il est quelqu'un sur terre; Eho! Eho!; Quand j'étais chez
    mon père
CHAUSSON: Le Colibri; Les Papillons; Le Temps des lilas
DE LARA: Rondel de l'adieu
DUPARC: Chanson triste; Le Manoir de Rosemonde; Phidylé; La Vie
    antérieure
RAVEL: Chants populaires; Nicolette
    Martial Singher, bar; Dorothy Angwin, pf

ARGO
ZK 28-29. *English Songs*
BENNETT: Tom O'Bedlams Song
BRIDGE: Goldenhair; Journey's End; So Perverse; 'Tis But a Week;
    When You Are Old
BUSCH: Come, O Come, My Life's Delight; The Echoing Green; If Thou
    Wilt Ease Thine Heart; The Shepherd
BUSH: Voices of the Prophets
DELIUS: To Daffodils
GRAINGER: Bold William Taylor
IRELAND: Friendship in Misfortune; The Land of Lost Content; Love and
    Friendship; The One Hope; The Trellis
MOERAN: The Merry Month of May
RAINIER: Cycle for Declamation
TIPPETT: Songs for Ariel
VAN DIEREN: Dream Pedlary; Take, O Take Those Lips Away
WARLOCK: Along the Stream; Piggesnie
        Peter Pears, ten; Benjamin Britten, pf; Viola Tunnard, pf;
        Joan Dickson, vlc

ZRG 638. *Lutyens and Bedford*
BEDFORD: Music for Albion Moonlight
LUTYENS: And Suddenly It's Evening
    Jane Manning, sop; Herbert Handt, ten; Members of the BBC Sym.,
    John Carewe

ZRG 5418. *Twentieth Century English Songs*
BENNETT: Tom O'Bedlams Song
BRIDGE: Goldenhair; Journey's End; So Perverse; 'Tis But a Week; When
    You Are Old
IRELAND: Friendship in Misfortune; The Land of Lost Content; Love and
    Friendship; The One Hope; The Trellis
RAINIER: Cycle for Declamation
    Peter Pears, ten; Benjamin Britten, pf; Joan Dickson, vlc

BRUNO WALTER SOCIETY
IGI-382. *Lieder*
MAHLER: Lieder eines fahrenden Gesellen
STRAUSS: Liebeshymnus; Verführung; Waldseligkeit; Winterliebe
WOLF: Anakreons Grab; Bedeckt mich mit Blumen; Im Frühling; Mögen alle
    bösen Zungen; Die Zigeunerin
        Dietrich Fischer-Dieskau, bar; Vienna Phil., Furtwängler; Peter
        Anders, ten; Berlin Phil., Furtwängler; Elisabeth Schwarzkopf, sop;
        Wilhelm Furtwängler, pf

CAMBRIDGE
CRS-2774. *Settings of Verlaine Poems*
DEBUSSY: C'est l'extase; Chevaux de bois; Clair de lune; En sourdine;
    Fantoches; Green; Il pleure dans mon coeur; Mandoline; L'Ombre des
    arbres; Spleen
DUPONT: Mandoline
FAURÉ: A Clymène; C'est l'extase; Clair de lune; En sourdine; Green;
    Mandoline; Spleen
SZULC: Clair de lune
    Carole Bogard, sop; John Moriarty, pf

CRS-2775. *French Songs*
BIZET: Berceuse; Chanson d'avril; Chant d'amour
CHABRIER: L'Île heureuse; Lied
FAURÉ: La Bonne Chanson
GOUNOD: Venise; Viens! Les Gazons sont verts
    Carole Bogard, sop; John Moriarty, pf

CAMBRIDGE—*continued*

2777. *Songs by Le Groupe des Six*
AURIC: Il était une petite pie; Les Pâquerettes; Une Petite Pomme; Les Petits Anes; La Poule noire; Printemps
DUREY: La Boule de neige; La Grenade; La Métempsychose
HONEGGER: Les Cloches; Clotilde; La Delphinium
MILHAUD: L'Aurore; Fête de Bordeaux; Fête de Montmartre; Fumée
POULENC: Air champêtre; Attributs; Chanson Bretonne; Hier; La Petite Servante; Le Tombeau
TAILLEFERRE: Chanson françaises
Carole Bogard, sop; John Moriarty, pf

CAPRICE

RIKS LP 59. *Dorothy Dorow and Friends*
BÄCK: Neither Nor
BELL: Grass
MAROS: Descort
MUSGRAVE: Primavera
NORGARD: Wenn die Rose sich selbst schmückt
WERLE: Now All the Fingers of This Tree
Dorothy Dorow, sop; Ensemble, Bell

CBS

36682. *Think on Me*
BRAHMS: Mein Mädel hat einen Rosenmund
DVORAK: Als die alte Mutter
GERSHWIN: By Strauss
GRANADOS: El majo discreto
GUASTAVINO: La rosa y el sauce
HAHN: Le Rossignol des lilas
LISZT: Es muss ein Wunderbares sein
MONTSALVATGE: Cancion de cuna para dormir a un negrito
NIN: Piano murciano
POULENC: Les Chemins de l'amour
SCOTT: Think on Me
TURINA: Las locos por amor
VAUGHAN WILLIAMS: Silent Noon
WAGNER: Träume
WECKERLIN: Tambourin
Elly Ameling, sop; Dalton Baldwin, pf

CETRA

LPO 2003. *Recital*

BELLINI: Dolente immagine di fille mia; Il fervido desiderio; Vaga luna che inargenti

CHOPIN: Melodie polacche

DONIZETTI: A mezzanotte; La corrispondenza amorosa; La Mère et l'enfant; La danza; L'orgia; La promessa

Leyla Gencer, m-sop; Marcello Guerrini, pf.

COLUMBIA

M-33933. *Plaisir d'amour*

BIZET: Ouvre ton coeur

DELIBES: Les Filles de Cadix

DELL'ACQUA: Villanelle

GOUNOD: Waltz (*Mireille*)

KOECHLIN: Si tu le veux

LENOIR: Parley-moi d'amour

LISZT: Oh! quand je dors

MARTINI: Plaisir d'amour

POULENC: Les Chemins de l'amour

Beverly Sills, sop; Columbia Sym. Orch., Kostelanetz

M-34501. *Serenata*

CATALANI: La notte è placida; Vieni! deh, vien

LEONCAVALLO: Sérénade française; Sérénade napolitaine

MASCAGNI: La luna; M'ama non m'ama; Serenata

PIZZETTI: I pastori

PUCCINI: Menti all'avviso; Sole e amore

RESPIGHI: Au milieu du jardin; Povero core; Razzolan; Soupir

TOSTI: Malia; La Serenata

WOLF-FERRARI: Il campiello

Renata Scotto, sop; John Atkins, pf

M-34518. *Scarlatti and Handel*

HANDEL: Care selve; Eternal Source of Light Divine; Let the Bright Seraphim; Lusinghe più care; Three instrumental pieces from ''A Choice Sett of Aires'': Allegro, Bourée, March

SCARLATTI: Contentatevi, o fidi pensieri; Dite almeno, astri crudeli; Infelici miei lumi; Su le sponde del Tebro; Tralascia pur di piangere

Judith Blegen, sop; Gerard Schwarz, tpt; Col. Chamber Orch., Schwarz

M-35119. *Souvenirs*

BRITTEN: O Waly, Waly

CANTELOUBE: Brezairola

HAHN: La Dernière Valse

COLUMBIA—*continued*
HULLEBROECK: Afrikaans Wiegeliedjie
IVES: Memories
LISZT: O Lieb, so lang du lieben kannst
MARTIN: Unter der Linden
NAKADA: Oyasumi na sai
PURCELL: Music for a While
RACHMANINOFF: Spring Waters
RODRIGO: De los álamos vengo, madre
ROSSINI: La danza
SCHOENBERG: Gigerlette
SIBELIUS: Varn flyktar hastigt
VUILLERMOZ: Jardin d'amour
 Elly Ameling, sop; Dalton Baldwin, pf.

M-35127. *Song Recital*
CANTELOUBE: Chants de France
DEBUSSY: Chansons de Bilitis
DOWLAND: Come Again, Sweet Love; Sorrow, Stay
HALL: Jenny Rebecca
LISZT: Die drei Zigeuner; Einst; Oh! quand je dors
PURCELL: The Blessed Virgin's Expostulation
 Frederica Von Stade, sop; Martin Katz, pf

M-35139. *Recital*
ALBENIZ: Six Songs to Italian Texts
BAUTISTA: Three Songs Dedicated to Andalusian Cities
MORENO: Four Aztec Songs
RODRIGO: Four Sephardic Songs
 Victoria de los Angeles, sop; Geoffrey Parsons, pf

36666. *Ravel and Satie*
RAVEL: Histoires naturelles
SATIE: Chanson du chat; Le Chapelier; Daphénéo; La Diva de l'Empire;
 Je te veux; L'Omnibus automobile; Le Statue de bronze; Tendrement
 Régine Crespin, sop; Philippe Entremont, pf

M-36667. *Song Recital*
DUPARC: Au pays où se fait la guerre; L'Invitation au voyage; Le Manoir de
 Rosemonde
FAURÉ: Aprés un rêve; Nell
SCHUBERT: Gretchen am Spinnrade; Nacht und Träume; Rastlose Liebe
SCHUMANN, Robert: Du bist wie eine Blume; Die Soldatenbraut; Stille Tränen
WALTON: Daphne; Old Sir Faulk; Through Gilded Trellises
WOLF: Blumengruss
 Kiri Te Kanawa, sop; Richard Amner, pf

M-37210. *Fauré and Debussy*
DEBUSSY: Ariette oubliées; Chansons de Bilitis
FAURÉ: La Bonne Chanson
    Elly Ameling, sop; Dalton Baldwin, pf

IM-37231. *Von Stade Live*
CANTELOUBE: L'aïo de rotso; Brezairola
COPLAND: Why Do They Shut Me Out of Heaven?
DURANTE: Danza, danza, fanciulla gentile
HUNDLEY: The Astronomers; Come Ready and See Me
MARCELLO: Il mio bel foco
RAVEL: Cinq Mélodies populaires grecques
SCARLATTI: Se tu della mia morte?
THOMSON: A Prayer to Saint Catherine
VIVALDI: Filli di gioa vuoi farmi morir
TRADITIONAL: The Leprechaun
    Frederica Von Stade, sop; Martin Katz, pf

COMPOSERS RECORDINGS, Inc. (CRI)

307. *Babbitt and Sessions*
BABBITT: Philomel
SESSIONS: Piano Sonata no. 3
    Bethany Beardslee, sop; syn. sound; Robert Helps, pf

SD-343. *American Contemporary Vocal Music*
GIDEON: The Condemned Playground; Questions on Nature
WEISGALL: End of Summer
    Phyllis Bryn-Julson, sop; Constantine Cassolas, ten; Felix Galimar,
    vln; Michael Tolomeo, vla; Fortunato Arico, vlc; Paul Dunkel, fl;
    Jack Shapiro, vln; Jan De Gaetani, m-sop; Charles Bressler, ten;
    chamber groups

SD-370. *Other Voices*
BLANK: Two Songs for Voice and Bassoon
SMIT: At the Corner of the Sky (choral); Songs of Wonder
WILSON: Sometimes
    William A. Brown, ten; Jan De Gaetani, m-sop; Martha Hanneman,
    sop; Arthur Weisberg, bsn; Leo Smit, pf; Choir of St. Paul's
    Cathedral, Buffalo, N.Y., Burgomaster

SD 379. *American Contemporary Voices and Instruments*
WERNICK: Haiku of Basho; Moonsongs from the Japanese
BOROS: Anecdote of the Jar (instrumental)
    Neva Pilgrim, sop; Cont. Chamber Players of Univ. of Chicago

COMPOSERS RECORDINGS, Inc. (CRI) —*continued*
SD 380. *American Contemporary Words and Music*
AHROLD: Three Poems of Sylvia Plath
ARGENTO: Six Elizabethan Songs
HERVING: Chamber Music for Six Players
> Barbara Martin, sop; Corrine Curry, m-sop; London Sym. Orch.,
> Farberman; chamber groups

SD 401. *Gideon and Boykan*
BOYKAN: Second String Quartet
GIDEON: Nocturnes; Songs of Youth and Madness
> Judith Raskin, sop; Da Capo Cham. Players, De Main; Amer.
> Composers Orch., Dixon; Pro Arte Quartet

S-420. *Music and Words*
ALBERT: To Wake the Dead
PERERA: Three Poems of Günter Grass
> Sheila Marie Allen, sop; Pro Musica Moderna, Fussell; Elsa
> Charlston, sop; Boston Musica Viva, Pittman

SD 426. *Voices and Instruments*
BAUR: The Moon and the Yew Trees
CHATMAN: Whisper Baby (choral)
RHODES: Visions of Remembrance (duet)
> Christine Anderson, sop; Carol Wilson, sop; Lorraine Manz, m-sop;
> instruments

437. *Wilson, Thome and Yannay*
THOME: Anaïs (instrumental)
WILSON: Eclogue (piano); The Ballad of Longwood Glen
YANNAY: At the End of the Parade
> Paul Sperry, ten; Nancy Allen, hp; Lawrence Weller, bar; Diane
> Thome, pf; Michael Finckel, vlc; Orch. of Our Time, Thome

453. *Starer and Perlongo*
PERLONGO: Ricercar; Fragments (instrumental)
STARER: Anna Margarita's Will
> Phyllis Bryn-Julson, sop; Karl Kraber, fl; Stephen Kates, vlc; Paul
> Ingraham, horn; Donald Sutherland, pf; Pittsburgh New Music
> Ensemble, Stock; James Walker, fl; Ronald Leonard, vlc

SD 462. *American Songs*
BACON: The Banks of the Yellow Sea; Eden; The Heart; I'm Nobody; Poor
Little Heart; Simple Days

BEACH: Ah, Love, But a Day; I Send My Heart Up to Thee; The Year's at
the Spring
BEESON: Death by Owl-Eyes; Eldorado; The You Should Of Done It Blues
HOIBY: Night Songs
WIESGALL: Four Songs on Poems by Adelaide Crapsey
Carolyn Heafner, sop; Dixie Ross Neill, pf

SD 466. *O'Brien and Peyton*
O'BRIEN: Embarking for Cythera; Allures (instrumental)
PEYTON: Songs from Walt Whitman
Bethany Beardslee, sop; Linda Quan, vln; Malcomb Peyton, pf;
instrumentalists

DECCA
ZRG 691. *Hoddinott and Tate*
HODDINOTT: Roman Dream; Trio for Violin, cello and piano
TATE: Apparitions; Three Gaelic Ballads
Margaret Price, sop; James Lockhart, pf; instrumentalists

SXL 6608. *Britten and Purcell*
BRITTEN: Tit for Tat; Who Are These Children?; Canticle IV (trio)
PURCELL: Sweeter than Roses; When the Cock Begins to Crow (trio)
James Bowman, ct-ten; Peter Pears, ten; John Shirley-Quirk, ten;
Benjamin Britten, pf

DESMAR
DSM 1010. *German Songs*
BRAHMS: Auf dem Kirchhofe; Meine Liebe ist grün; Nachtigall; Therese;
Der Tod, das ist die kühle Nacht; Vergebliches Ständchen
MOZART: Als Luise die Briefe; Un moto do gioia; Das Veilchen; Der
Zauberer
SCHUBERT: An die Nachtigall; Heidenröslein; Nacht und Träume; Rastlose
Liebe
WOLF: Italienisches Liederbuch (excerpts)
Benita Valente, sop; Richard Goode, pf

DEUTSCHE GRAMMOPHON
2530 598. *Canciones españolas*
ANCHIETA: Con amores, la mi madre
ESTEVE: Alma, sintamos!
GRANADOS: Il majo discreto; La maja dolorosa; El majo timido; El tra la la y
el punteado

DEUTSCHE GRAMMOPHON—*continued*
GURIDI: Seis canciones castellanas
MONTSALVATGE: Cinco canciones negras
TORRE: Pámpano verde
TURINA: Cantares; El Fantasma; Saeta
Teresa Berganza, m-sop; Felix Lavilla, pf

2530 875. *Canciones populares españolas*
FALLA: Siete canciones populares españolas
GARCIA LORCA: Trece canciones españolas antiguas
Teresa Berganza, m-sop; Narciso Yepes, gtr

2531 192. *Italian Baroque Songs*
CALDARA: Come raggio di sol; Selve amiche
CARISSIMI: No, non si speri; Vittoria, mio cuore
CAVALLI: Son ancor pargoletta
PERGOLESI: Confusa, smarrita; Se tu m'ami
SCARLATTI: Se delitto è l'adorarti; Se Florindo è fedele; Le violette
VIVALDI: Un certo non so che; Piango, gemo, sospiro
Teresa Berganza, m-sop; Ricardo Requejo, pf

DISCOPHILIA
KG-G-4. *Lieder Recital*
BRAHMS: Der Ganz zur Liebchen; Therese; Der Tod, das ist die kühle
Nacht; Zigeunerlieder
SCHUBERT: Dithyrambe; Ellens zweiter Gesang; Die Stadt; Wiegenlied
WOLF: Der Mond hat eine schwere Klag erhoben; Und willst du deinen
Liebsten
Elena Gerhardt, sop; instruments

ECLIPSE
ECS 545. *An English Song Recital*
BERKELEY: How Love Came In
BRIDGE: Go Not, Happy Day; Love Went A-Riding
BRITTEN: Let the Florid Music Praise
BUTTERWORTH: Is My Team Ploughing?
DOWLAND: Awake, Sweet Love; In Darkness Let Me Dwell
FORD: Fair, Sweet, Cruel
HOLST: Persephone
IRELAND: I Have Twelve Oxen
MOERAN: In Youth Is Pleasure
MORLEY: Come Sorrow, Come; Mistress Mine, Well May You Fare

OLDHAM: Three Chinese Lyrics
ROSSETER: What Then Is Love but Mourning; When Laura Smiles
WARLOCK: Yarmouth Fair
    Peter Pears, ten; Benjamin Britten, pf; Julian Bream, lute

ELECTROLA (EMI)

EMI 063-02375. *Ein Liederabend* (also issued as ASD 2902, *Favourite Songs and Encores*)
BACH: Bist du bei mir
BEETHOVEN: Wonne der Wehmut
BRAHMS: Da unten im Tale
CHAUSSON: Le Colibri; Les Papillons
DUPARC: Chanson triste
FAURÉ: Après un rêve
GRIEG: Ich liebe dich
HAHN: Si mes vers avaient des ailes
HAYDN: Mermaid's Song
LOEWE: Niemand hat's gesehn
MARCHESI: La folletta
MENDELSSOHN: Auf Flügeln des Gesanges
SATIE: La Diva de l'Empire; Je te veux
SCARLATTI: Le violette
SCHUBERT: Seligkeit
STRAVINSKY: Pastorale
    Elly Ameling, sop; Dalton Baldwin, pf

1C 065-45 418. *Strauss and Schumann*
SCHUMANN, Robert: Heiss mich nicht reden; Mignon; Nur wer die Sehnsucht kennt; Requiem; Singet nicht in Trauertönen; So lasst mich scheinen, bis ich werde; Stille Tränen
STRAUSS: Befreit; Drei Lieder der Ophelia aus ''Hamlet''; Frühlingsfeier; Schlechtes Wetter; Ständchen
    Edda Moser, sop; Irwin Gage, pf

EMI 1C 065-46 356. *Debussy and Schoenberg*
DEBUSSY: Ariettes oubliées; Fêtes galantes I, II
SCHOENBERG: Das Buch der hängenden Gärten
    Charlotte Lehmann, sop; Werner Genuit, pf

EMI SLS 5055. *Russian Songs*
MUSSORGSKY: Darling Savishna; Eremushka's Lullaby; Hopak; The Orphan; Peasant's Lullaby; ''Sunless'' Cycle; Where Art Thou Little Star?
SHOSTAKOVICH: Satires; Seven Poems

ELECTROLA (EMI)—*continued*
   TCHAIKOVSKY: Again, as Before; Cradle Song; Do Not Believe, My Dear; The Fearful Minute; If I'd Only Known; In This Moonlight; It Was in the Early Spring; Mid the Din of the Ball; Sleep, My Poor Friend; Was I Not a Little Blade of Grass?; Why?
         Galina Vishnevskaya, sop; Mstislav Rostropovitch, pf, vln; Ulf Hoelscher, vln; Vasso Devetzi, pf

GRENADILLA
   GS-1015. *The Jubal Trio*
   JOLLES: Wordsworth Songs
   MAMLOK: Haiku Settings
   SCHICKELE: The Lowest Trees Have Tops
         Lucy Shelton, sop; Sue Ane Kahn, fl; Susan Jolles, hp; John Graham, vla

   GS-1029/30. *The Cantilena Chamber Players*
   AMRAM: Portraits
   FELDMAN: Four Instruments
   HADJU: Five Sketches in a Sentimental Mood
   KOPYTMAN: About an Old Tune
   KUPFERMAN: Abracadabra
   ORGAD: Shaar, Shaar
   PARTOS: Piano Quartet
   SIEGMEISTER: Songs of Experience
         Elaine Bonazzi, m-sop; Harry Zaratzian, vla; Frank Glazer, pf; Edna Michell, vln; Stephen Kates, vlc.

HNH
   4008. *Arias and Songs of the Italian Baroque*
   CALDARA: Vaghe luci
   DURANTE: Danza, danza, fanciulla gentile
   GIORDANI: Caro mio ben
   PERGOLESI: Tre giorni son che Nina
   SCARLATTI: O cessate di piagarmi; Già il sole dal Gange; Su, venite a consiglio; Toglietemi la vita ancor; Le violette
   VIVALDI: Dille ch'il viver mio; O di tua man mi svena; Se cerca, se dice
         Carlo Berganzi, ten; Felix Lavilla, pf

   4045. *Fauré, Ravel and Poulenc*
   FAURÉ: La Bonne Chanson
   POULENC: Le Bal masqué

RAVEL: Chansons madécasses
Dietrich Fischer-Dieskau, bar; Members of the Berlin Phil.; Wolfgang
Sawallisch, pf

HUNGAROTON
SLPX-12406. *Lieder Recital*
BRAHMS: Dein blaues Augen; Ständchen
DEBUSSY: Chansons de Bilitis
KODALY: Mónár Anna; Nausikaa
SCHUBERT: An den Mond; Erlkönig; Der Musensohn
STRAUSS: Allerseelen; Du meines Herzens Krönelein; Wie sollten wir
geheim sie halten
Julia Hamari, sop; Emmi Varasdy, pf

LEONARDA
LPI 106. *Song Cycles for Soprano Plus*
SCHONTHAL: Totengesänge
WEILL: Frauentanz
ZAIMONT: Two Songs for Soprano and Harp
Edith Gorgon Ainsberg, sop; Bernice Bramson, sop; Sara Cutler, hp;
Ruth Schonthal, pf; Bronx Arts Ensemble

LPI 107. *Lieder*
HENSEL, Fanny Mendelssohn: Du bist die Ruh; Im Herbste; Nachtwanderer;
Die Nonne; Der Rosenkranz; Vorwurf
LANG: Frühzeitiger Frühling; O sehntest du dich so nach mir; Wie gläntz
so hell dein Auge; Wie, wenn die Sonn' aufgeht; Der Winter
SCHUMANN, Clara: Das ist ein Tag, der klingen mag; Er ist gekommen
in Sturm und Regen; Ich stand in dunklen Träumen; Liebst du um
Schönheit; Die stille Lotusblume; Warum willst du and're tragen; Was
weinst du, Blümlein
VIARDOT-GARCIA: Die Beschwörung; Des Nachts; Das Vöglein
Katherine Ciesinski, m-sop; John Ostendorf, bs-bar; Rudolph
Palmer, pf.

LPI 112. *Recital*
HENSEL, Fanny Mendelssohn: Gondellied; Mayenlied; Morgenständchen;
Schwanenlied; Wanderlied; Warum sind denn die Rosen so blass
REICHARDT: Bergmannslied; Betteley der Vögel; Die Blume der Blumen;
Duettino; Heimweh; Hier liegt ein Spielmann begraben; Tre canzoni
SCHUBERT: Die schöne Müllerin
Grayson Hirst, ten; Michel Yuspeh, pf

LONDON
   OSA-13132. *Serate musicali*
   ADAM: Mariquita
   BELLINI: Che inargenti; Dolente immagine di fille mia; Malinconia ninfa
   gentile; Vaga luna che inargenti
   BIZET: Pastorale
   CAMPANA: L'ultime speme
   CHAMINADE: Berceuse
   CIMARA: Stornello
   DALAYRAC: Quand le bienaimé reviendra
   DAVID: Les Hirondelles
   DELIBES: Les Filles de Cadix
   DONIZETTI: J'attend toujours; A mezzanotte; Il sospiro
   FAURÉ: Le Papillon et la fleur
   GODARD: Chanson de Florian
   GOUNOD: Au printemps
   LALO: L'Esclave
   LEONCAVALLO: Serenade française
   MASCAGNI: La tua stella
   MASSENET: Oh, si les fleurs avaient des yeux; Pensée d'automne;
   Puisqu'elle à pris ma vie
   MEYERBEER: Guide au bord ta nacelle
   PONCHIELLI: Il Trovatore
   RESPIGHI: I tempi assai lontani
   ROSSINI: Les Adieux à la vie; Arietta all'antica; Chanson de Zora; Soirées
   musicales
   SAINT-SAËNS: Aimons-nous
   THOMAS: Le Soir
   VERDI: Il poveretto
         Joan Sutherland, sop; Richard Bonynge, pf

   R 23219. *A Recital of Songs and Arias*
   ANON: Leggiadro occhi belli
   BELLINI: Dolente immagine de fille mia; Vanne, O rosa fortunata
   FAVARA: A la barcillunisa
   HANDEL: Piangerò la sorte mia
   MARTUCCI: Al folto bosco; Cantava il ruscello; Passo e non ti vedo;
   Sur mar al navicella
   ROSSINI: La promessa
   SARTI: Lungi dal caro bene
   SCARLATTI: Le violette
   TURINA: Cantares
   VERDI: Stornello
         Renata Tebaldi, sop; Giorgio Favaretto, pf

OS-26302. *German Lieder*
SCHUBERT: Fischerweise; Im Frühling; Die junge Nonne; Nacht und Träume
SCHUMANN, Robert: Abendlied; Aus den hebräischen Gesängen; Die
Kartenlegerin; Die Lotusblume
STRAUSS: Befreit; Für fünfzehn Pfennige; Schön sind, doch kalt
WOLF: Auf einer Wanderung; Der Genesene an die Hoffnung; Mein
Liebster; Mignon
Marilyn Horne, m-sop; Martin Katz, pf

OS 26376. *Eighteenth Century Arias*
BONONCINI: Deh più a me non v'ascondete
GLUCK: O del mio dolce ardor; Divinités du Styx
HANDEL: Ombra mai fù; Verdi prati
MARTINI: Plaisir d'amour
PAISIELLO: Chi vuol la zingarella; La molinara; Nel cor più mi sento;
I zingari in Fiera
PERGOLESI: Stizzoso, mio stizzoso; Tre giorni son che Nina
SARTI: Lungi dal caro bene
SCARLATTI: Le violette
VIVALDI: Piango, gemo, sospiro
Renata Tebaldi, sop; New Phil. Orch., Bonynge

OS 26391. *Pavarotti in Concert*
BELLINI: Bella Nice che d'amore; Dolente immagine de fille mia; Malinconia
ninfa gentile; Ma rendi pur contento; Vanne, O rose fortunata
BONONCINI: Per la gloria
HANDEL: Care selve
RESPIGHI: Nebbie; Nevicata; Pioggia
ROSSINI: La danza
SCARLATTI: Già il sole dal Gange
TOSTI: Luna d'estate; Malia; Non t'amo più; La serenata
Luciano Pavarotti, ten; Orch. del Teatro Comunale di Bologna,
Bonynge

OS 26575. *Seven Popular Spanish Songs*
FALLA: Siete canciones populares españolas
GRANADOS: Cancó d'amor; Elegia eterna; La maja y el ruisenor; L'ocell
profeta
TURINA: Anhelos; Cantares; Farruca; Si con mis deseos
Montserrat Caballé, sop; Miguel Zanetti, pf

OS 26592. *To My Friends*
BRAHMS: Blinde Kuh; Mädchenlied; Therese
GRIEG: Ein Schwann
LOEWE: Die wandelnde Glocke

LONDON—*continued*

WOLF: Auf ein altes Bild; Bei einer Trauung; Elfenlied; Fussreise; Heimweh; Jägerlied; Lebe wohl; Mausfallen-Sprüchlein; Nimmersatte Liebe; Nixe Binsefuss; Selbstgeständnis; Storchenbotschaft; Das verlassene Mägdlein
Elisabeth Schwarzkopf, sop; Goeffrey Parsons, pf

OS 26617. *Song Recital*
ALBENIZ: Besa el aura; Del salón
FALLA: Oracion de las Madres que tienen a sus hijos en brazos; Tus ojillos negros
GRANADOS: La maja dolorosa
OBRADORS: Aquel sombrero de monte; Del cabello más sutil; El molondrón; El vito
RODRIGO: Cuatro madrigales amatorios
VIVES: El amor y los ojos; El retrato de Isabela; Válgame Dios, que los ansares vuelan
Montserrat Caballé, sop; Manuel Zanetti, pf

OS 26618. *Arie antiche*
COSTANZI: Lusinga la speme
GIORDANI: Caro mio ben
LOTTI: Pur dicesti, o bocca bella
MARCELLO: Quella fiamma che m'accende
PAISIELLO: Nel cor più non mi sento
PERGOLESI: Se tu m'ami
VIVALDI: Agitata da due venti; sposa son disprezzata; Vieni, vieni, o mio diletto
Montserrat Caballé, sop; Miguel Zanetti, pf

MUSICAL HERITAGE SOCIETY

MHS 1976. *Music for Voice and Violin*
BLACHER: Francesca di Rimini
HOLST: Four Songs for Voice and Violin
HOVHANESS: Hercules
VAUGHAN WILLIAMS: Along the Field
VILLA-LOBOS: Suite for Voice and Violin
Catherine Malfitano, sop; Joseph Malfitano, vln

MHS 3770. *Songs of the Great Opera Composers,* volume II
BARBER: I Hear an Army; Nocturne; A Nun Takes the Veil; Rain Has Fallen; The Secrets of the Old; Sleep Now; Solitary Hotel; Sure on This Shining Night; With Rue My Heart Is Laden
BERG: Seven Early Songs
Joan Patenaude, sop; Mikael Eliasen, pf

MHS 4531. *An Album of English Songs*
BRITTEN: Winter Words
BUSH: Echo's Lament for Narcissus; The Wonder of Wonders
GIBBS: The Fields Are Full; A Song of Shadows
GURNEY: Nine of the Clock; Ploughman Singing; Under the Greenwood Tree
HOLST: The Floral Bandit; A Little Music; The Thought
QUILTER: Go, Lovely Rose; O Mistress Mine
WARLOCK: As Ever I Saw; To the Memory of a Great Singer
     Ian Partridge, ten; Jennifer Partridge, pf

NEW WORLD RECORDS
NW 243. *But Yesterday Is Not Today*
BARBER: Sure on This Shining Night
BOWLES: Once a Lady Was Here; Song of an Old Woman
CHANLER: The Children; Moo Is a Cow; Once Upon a Time; The Rose;
    These, My Ophelia; Thomas Logge
CITKOWITZ: Five Songs from "Chamber Music"
COPLAND: Song
DUKE: Luke Havergal; Miniver Cheevy; Richard Cory
HELPS: The Running Sun
       Bethany Beardslee, sop; Robert Helps, pf; Donald Gramm, bar;
       Donald Hassard, pf

NW 300. *Anthology of American Music*
CHANLER: Four Rhymes from 'Peacock Pie"
DELLO JOIO: The Listeners
FINE: Four Songs from "Childhood Fables for Grownups"
IVES: At the River; The Camp Meeting; Chanson de Florian; Elegie; His
    Exaltation; Qu'il m'irait; Rosamunde; Sunrise; Watchman
WARD: Ballad from "Pantaloon"
       William Parker, bar; Dalton Baldwin, pf; Ani Kavafian, vl

NW 305. *An American Song Recital*
BACON: Billy in the Darbies
EVETT: Billy in the Darbies
GRIFFES: Das ist ein Brausen und Heulen; Des Müden Abendlied; The First
    Snowfall; An Old Song Resung; Wo ich bin, mich rings umdunkelt; Zwei
    Könige
HOIBY: Anatomy Lesson from "Summer and Smoke"
NILES: Evening; For My Brother, Reported Missing in Action, 1943; Love
    Winter when the Plant Says Nothing
ROREM: Mourning Scene
       William Parker, bar; William Huckaby, pf; Virgil Blackwell, cl; Col.
       String Quartet

NONESUCH

H-71320. *Schoenberg and Schubert*
SCHOENBERG: Das Buch der hängenden Gärten
SCHUBERT: An mein Herz; Blondel zu Marien; Ganymed; Heidenröslein; Der
Musensohn; Rastlose Liebe; Schäfers Klaglied; Sprache der Liebe
Jan De Gaetani, m-sop; Gilbert Kalish, pf

H-71342. *Davies and Wernick*
DAVIES: Dark Angels
WERNICK: Songs of Remembrance
Jan De Gaetani, m-sop; Oscar Ghiglia, gtr; Philip West, shawm,
Eng. horn

H-71373. *Songs*
CHAUSSON: Amour d'antan; La Caravane; Le Charme; Le Colibri; Les
Papillons; Le Temps des lilas
RACHMANINOFF: The Answer; The Harvest of Sorrow; How Long since
Love; Lilacs; Oh, Do Not Grieve; A Passing Breeze; To the Children;
Christ Is Risen
Jan De Gaetani, m-sop; Gilbert Kalish, pf

NORTHEASTERN RECORDS

NR 201. *Love Can Be Still*
PINKHAM: Three Choral Works
SNYDER: Love Is a Language
Richard Conrad, ten; Patti Dell, sop; Pamela Gore, alto; Bryan
McNeil, bar; Barbara Wallace, sop; Elena Gambulos, sop; Donald
Palumbo, pf

ODEON

C 063 00391. *Lieder Recital*
SCHUBERT: Abendstern; Am Grabe Anselmos; Auflösung; Der
Gondelfahrer; Die Götter Griechenlands; Die Vögel
STRAUSS: Allerseelen; All' mein Gedanken; Befreit; Heimliche
Aufforderung; Morgen; Die Nacht; Wiegenlied
WOLF: Ach, des Knaben Augen; Die ihr schwebet; Herr, was trägt der
Boden hier; Nun wandre Maria
Janet Baker, m-sop; Gerald Moore, pf

C 06502673. *Lieder der Schumannianer*
FRANZ: Abends; Auf dem Meere (3 versions); Bitte; Für Musik; Gewitter-
nacht; Mailied; Wie des Mondes Abbild; Wonne der Wehmut
GRIEG: Abschied; Dereinst, Gedanke mein; Hör' ich das Liedchen klingen;
Jägerlied; Lauf der Welt; Morgentau; Wo sind sie hin?

HILLER: Gebet
JENSEN: Lehn deine Wang' an meine Wang'
KIRCHNER: Frühlingslied (3 versions); Sie weiss es nicht
RUBENSTEIN: Es blinket der Tau
    Dietrich Fischer-Dieskau, bar; Aribert Reimann, pf

C 06502674. *Lieder der Neudeutschen*
BERLIOZ: Auf den Lagunen
CORNELIUS: Liebe ohne Heimat; Sonnenuntergang
EULENBURG: Liebessehnsucht
LISZT: Es rauschen die Winde; Ständchen; Über allen Gipfeln ist Ruh';
    Wieder möcht'ich dir begegnen
NIETZSCHE: Nachspiel; Verwelkt; Wie Rebenranken schwingen
RAFF: Unter den Palmen
RITTER: Primula veris
SCHILLINGS: Freude soll in deinen Werken sein
STREICHER: Ist dir ein getreues, liebevolles Kind beschert
WAGNER: Der Tannenbaum
WEINGARTNER: Liebesfeier
    Dietrich Fischer-Dieskau, bar; Aribert Reimann, pf

C 06502675. *Lieder der Jahrhundertwende*
MATTIESEN: Heimgang in der Frühe; Herbstgefühl
PFITZNER: An den Mond; Mailied
REGER: Sommernacht; Warnung
SCHOECK: Abendwolken; Reiselied
SCHREKER: Die Dunkelheit sinkt schwer wie Blei
STRAUSS: Wer hat's getan
TIESSEN: Vöglein Schwermut
WETZEL: An meine Mutter; Der Kehraus
    Dietrich Fischer-Dieskau, bar; Aribert Reimann, pf

C 06502676. *Aufbruch des 20. Jahrhunderts im Lied*
BARTÓK: Im Tale
BLACHER: Aprèslude
DEBUSSY: Pour ce que plaisance est morte; Le Temps a laissié son manteau
FORTNER: Abbitte; Hyperions Schicksalslied; Lied vom Weidenbaum
HINDEMITH: Fragment
MAHLER: Wo die schönen Trompeten blasen
MILHAUD: Lamentation
PFITZNER: Hussens Kerker
REUTTER: Johann Kepler; Lied für ein dunkles Mädchen; Trommel
SCHOECK: Peregrina
    Dietrich Fischer-Dieskau, bar; Hermann Reutter, pf

ODEON—*continued*

C 06502677. *Wirkung der neuen Wiener Schule im Lied*
APOSTEL: Nacht
BECK: Herbst
DESSAU: Noch bin ich eine Stadt; Sucht nicht mehr, Frau
EINEM: In der Fremde; Ein junger Dichter denkt an die Geliebte
EISLER: An die Hoffnung; In der Frühe; Spruch
HAUER: An die Parzen; Der gefesselte Strom
KRENEK: Erinnerung; Die frühen Gräber
SCHOENBERG: Traumleben; Warnung
WEBERN: Erwachen aus dem tiefsten Traumesschosse; Kunftag I; Das lockere Saatgefilde lechzet krank; Trauer I
    Dietrich Fischer-Dieskau, bar; Aribert Reimann, pf

2C 069-14089. *Mélodies françaises*
DEBUSSY: Aimon-nous et dormons; Jane; Quatres chansons de Jeunesse; Rondel chinois
FAURÉ: Arpège; Aurore; Lydia; Notre amour
GOUNOD: Chanson de printemps; La Naïade; O ma belle rebelle; Sérénade
HAHN: Infidélité; Néère; Trois Jours de vendanges; Tyndaris
    Mady Mesplé, sop; Janine Reiss, pf

ODYSSEY

Y 33130. *French Arias and Songs*
AUBER: L'Éclat de rire
CAMPRA: Chanson du papillon
CHOPIN: Tristesse
DEBUSSY: Air de Lia; De fleurs; Je voudrais qu'il fut
DUPARC: Chanson triste
HAHN: Si mes vers avaient des ailes
KOECHLIN: Si tu le veux
MORET: Le Nélumbo
RAVEL: Toi, le coeur de la rose
    Bidú Sayao, sop; Milne Charnley, pf; Col. Concert Orch., Breisach; Philadelphia Orch., Ormandy

OPUS ONE

13. *Recital*
BEHRENS: The Feast of Life
GILBERT: Poem VI, VII
ROBB: Dialogue
SHIELDS: Wildcat Songs
    Stephanie Turash, sop; instrumental ensemble

62. *Polin, Zahler and Edwards*
EDWARDS: Veined Variety
POLIN: O Aderyn Pur
ZAHLER: Regions I
    Johana Arnold, sop; instrumentalists

ORION
ORS-75174. *Chabrier and Liszt*
CHABRIER: Ballade des Gros Dindons; Chanson pour Jeanne; Les Cigales;
L'Île heureuse; Lied; Pastorale des petits cochons roses; Villanelle des
petits canards
LISZT: Anfangs wollt ich fast verzagen; Die drei Zigeuner; Ihr Auge; Die
Loreley; Kling leise, mein Lied; Über allen Gipfeln ist Ruh'; Vergiftet sind
meine Lieder; Wieder möcht'ich dir begegnen
    Paul Sperry, ten; Irma Vallecillo, pf

77272. *Recital*
CARPENTER: Gitanjali
GRIFFES: Evening Song; In a Myrtle Shade; Thy Dark Eyes to Mine; Waikiki
MacDOWELL: Confidence; Folksong; Fra Nightingale; Midsummer Lullaby;
The Swan; To a Wild Rose
    Alexandra Hunt, sop; Regis Benoit, pf

ORS 77280. *Recital*
GLUCK: O del mio dolce ardor
HANDEL: Ah, mio cor
RESPIGHI: Il tramonto
VIVALDI: Col piacer della mia fede; Sposa, son disprezzata
    Cathryn Ballinger, m-sop; I Virtuosi de Los Angeles, Cajati

ORS 78307. *Portrayals of Love in Italian Song*
BELLINI: Il fervido desiderio; Vaga luna che inargenti
MONTEVERDI: Ahi troppo duro; Quel sguardo sdegnosetto
PIZZETTI: Donna Lombarda; Levommi il mio pensier; La pesca dell'anello;
La prigioniera; Quel rossignol
ROSSINI: La gita in gondola; La promessa; Il rimprovero
    Anna Gabrieli, sop; Piotr Wolny, pf

ORS 78312. *Debussy and Ravel*
DEBUSSY: Aquarelles; Chevaux de bois; Colloque sentimental; Fantoches;
Le Jet d'eau; Mandoline; Trois Chansons de France
RAVEL: Chanson de Rouet; Epigramme de Cl. Marot; Les Grands Vents;
Manteau de fleurs; Noël des jouets; Rêves; Ronsard à son âme; Sainte;
Sur l'herbe
    Yolanda Marcoulescou, sop; Katja Phillabaum, pf

ORION—*continued*

81411. *The Ariel Ensemble*
BARAB: Bits and Pieces
GOTTLIEB: Downtown Blues for Uptown Halls
SCHUBERT: Der Hirt auf dem Felsen
STARER: The Ideal Self
VAUGHAN WILLIAMS: Three Vocalises
    Julia Lovett, sop; Jerome Bunke, cl; Michael Fardink, pf

ORS 82422. *Mélodies*
BERGER: Cinq Chansons (*Mary Stuart*)
MARTIN: Quatre Sonnets à Cassandre
MILHAUD: Six Chansons de théatre
POULENC: Deux Mélodies; La Fraîcheur et le feu; Quatre Poèmes
    d'Apollinaire
SATIE: Ludions
    Carol Kimball, m-sop; Thomas Grubb, pf; instruments

PATHÉ

2C 069-14044. *Bergerettes et Pastourelles*
SIMON: Il pleut bergère
WECKERLIN: Bergerettes; Pastourelles
    Mady Mesplé, sop; Janine Reiss, hpschd

PEARL

SHE 524. *Fauré and Duparc*
DUPARC: Chanson triste; Extase; Phidylé; Testament
FAURÉ: Aprés un rêve; Aubade; Aurore; Barcarolle; Chanson d'amour; Clair
    de lune; En prière; Nell; Poème d'un jour; Le Secret
    Ian Partridge, ten; Jennifer Partridge, pf

PELICAN

LP 2009. *Farewell Recital*
CORNELIUS: Ein Ton; Wiegenlied
FRANZ: Dies und Das; Für Musik; Gute Nacht; Ständchen; Weisst du noch
MENDELSSOHN: Der Mond; Venetianisches Gondellied
SCHUBERT: An die Musik; Danksagung an den Bach; Des Baches
    Wiegenlied; Die liebe Farbe; Der Neugierige; Tränenregen; Wohin
SCHUMANN, Robert: Alte Leute; O, ihr Herren; Ständchen; Widmung
WAGNER: Träume
    Lotte Lehmann, sop; Paul Ulanowsky, pf

PETERS INTERNATIONAL
PLE 136/7. *English Songs*
DELIUS: The Birds' Story; Hidden Love; The Homeward Way; The
Nightingale; Twilight Fancies; Young Venevil
GURNEY: All Night under the Moon; Bread and Cherries; Brown Is My Love;
The Cloths of Heaven; Desire in Spring; Down by the Salley Gardens;
An Epitaph; The Fields Are Full; The Folly of Being Comforted; Severn
Meadows; The Singer; Snow
VAUGHAN WILLIAMS: A Clear Midnight; Four Nights; How Can the Tree
but Wither?; Joy, Shipmate, Joy!; Motion and Stillness; The New Ghost;
Nocturne; The Twilight People; The Water Mill
WARLOCK: After Two Years; Away to Twiver; Balulalow; The Frostbound
Wood; Jillian of Berry; My Own Country; Passing By; Pretty Ring Time;
Rest, Sweet Nymphs; Sleep; Sweet-and-Twenty; Yarmouth Fair
Ian Partridge, ten; Jennifer Partridge, pf

PHILIPS
6500 706. *Lieder Recital*
SCHUBERT: An die Nachtigall; Fischerweise; Die Gebüsche; Im Freien;
Im Haine; Das Lied im Grünen; Der Schmetterling; Die Vögel; Der
Wachtelschlag
SCHUMANN, Robert: Frauenliebe und Leben
Elly Ameling, sop; Dalton Baldwin, pf

9500 350. *German Romantic Songs*
BRAHMS: Och Moder, ich well en Ding han; Schwesterlein
FRANZ: Aus meinen grossen Schmerzen
LOEWE: Der Fischer
MAHLER: Ablösung in Sommer
MENDELSSOHN: Die Liebende schreibt
PFITZNER: Ist der Himmel darum im Lenz so blau
REGER: Waldeinsamkeit
SCHUBERT: Du bist die Ruh; Nachtviolen
SCHUMANN, Robert: Der Nussbaum; Widmung
STRAUSS: Allerseelen; Hat gesagt; Ständchen; Traum durch die
Dämmerung
WOLF: Der Gärtner; Wiegenlied im Sommer
Elly Ameling, sop; Dalton Baldwin, pf

9500 356. *French Songs*
DUPARC: Chanson triste; L'Invitation au voyage; Phidylé; La Vie antérieure
POULENC: Les Chemins de l'amour; Le Grenouillère; Montparnasse; Voyage
à Paris

PHILIPS—*continued*
 RAVEL: Deux Mélodies hebraïque
 SATIE: Le Chapelier; Daphénéo; Je te veux; Le Statue de bronze
   Jessye Norman, sop; Dalton Baldwin, pf

9500 557. *Arie amorose*
 BONONCINI: Deh più a me non v'ascondete
 CACCINI: Amarilli, mia bella
 CALDARA: Come raggio di sol; Sebben crudele; Selve amiche
 CESTI: Intorno all'idol mio
 DURANTE: Danza, danza, fanciulla gentile
 GIORDANI: Caro mio ben
 LOTTI: Pur dicesti, o bocca bella
 MARTINI: Plaisir d'amour
 PAISIELLO: Nel cor più non mi sento
 PERGOLESI: Ogni pena più spietata
 PICCINNI: O notte o dea del mistero
 SARTI: Sen corre l'agnelletta
 SCARLATTI: Già il sole dal Gange; Sento nel core; Spesso vibra per suo gioco
 STRADELLA: Ragion sempre addita
   Janet Baker, m-sop; instrumentalists; Academy of St. Martin-in-the-Fields, Marriner

RCA
 ARLI-1281. *Music for Voice and Guitar*
 BRITTEN: I Will Give My Love an Apple; Master Kilby; Sailor-Boy; Second Lute Song from *Gloriana*; The Shooting of His Dear; The Soldier and the Sailor; Songs from the Chinese
 FRICKER: O Mistress Mine
 SEIBER: Four French Folk Songs
 WALTON: Fain Would I Change That Note; I Gave Her Cakes and I Gave Her Ale; Lady, When I Behold the Roses; My Love in Her Attire; O Stay, Sweet Love, To Couple Is a Custom
   Peter Pears, ten; Julian Brean, gtr

 AGLI-1341. *Songs*
 BELLINI: Dolente immagine di fille mia; Malinconia ninfa gentile; Per pietà bell'idol mio; Vaga luna che inargenti
 DONIZETTI: La corrispondenza amoroso; Una lagrima; La Mère et l'enfant; Ne ornera la bruna chioma
 ROSSINI: La danza; Giovanna d'Arco
 VERDI: Brindisi; Lo spazzacamino; Stornello
   Renata Scotto, sop; Walter Baracchi, pf

ARLI-1571. *Strauss and Wolf*
STRAUSS: Amor; Heimkehr; Ich schwebe; Ich wollt ein Sträusslein binden;
Säusle, liebe Myrtle; Schlagende Herzen; Der Stern
WOLF: Ach, des Knaben Augen; Die Bekehrte; Die ihr schwebet;
Epiphanias; Nun wandre Maria; Schlafendes Jesuskind; Die Spröde;
Verschwiegene Liebe; Waldmädchen; Zum neuen Jahr
    Judith Blegen, sop; Martin Katz, pf

ARLI-3022. *Schubert and Brahms Lieder*
BRAHMS: Botschaft; Dein blaues Augen; Der Schmied; Vergebliches
Ständchen; Von ewiger Liebe
SCHUBERT: An die Musik; Erlkönig; Die Forelle; Gretchen am Spinnrade;
Heidenröslein; Liebesbotschaft; Suleika; Der Tod und das Mädchen;
Ungeduld; Wiegenlied
    Marian Anderson, con; Franz Rupp, pf

ROCOCO
5365. *Reynaldo Hahn and His Songs*
BIZET: Chanson d'avril; O Nadir (*Pêcheur de perles*)
CHABRIER: Les Cigales; L'Île heureuse; Toutes les fleurs
GOUNOD: Biondina bella
HAHN: L'Enamourée; Etudes latines-Phillis; L'Heure exquise; Je me mets
en votre mercy; Offrande; Paysage triste; Le plus beau présent; Le
Temps d'aimer (Le Chien fidèle); Lettre d'amour; Venezia-Chè pecà
LULLY: Bois épais
PALADILHE: Psyché
    Arthur Endrèze, bar; Guy Ferrant, bar; Reynaldo Hahn, bar and pf

SAGA
5388. *A Recital of French Songs*
BERLIOZ: La Belle Voyageuse; Le Coucher du soleil; L'Origine de la harpe
BIZET: Adieux de l'hôtesse Arabe; Chanson d'avril; La Chanson de la rose;
Vous ne priez pas
DEBUSSY: Noël des enfants qui n'ont plus de maisons; Proses lyriques
    Jill Gomez, sop; John Constable, pf

5409. *A Recital of Spanish Songs*
FALLA: Siete canciones populares españolas; Trois Mélodies
GRANADOS: Coleccion de tonadillas
TURINA: Poema en forma de canciones
    Jill Gomez, sop; John Constable, pf

SERAPHIM

S-60251. *Lieder and Chansons*
DEBUSSY: Green; Beau Soir
DUPARC: L'Invitation au voyage; Phidylé
FAURÉ: Les Berceaux; La Chanson du pêcheur; Mai
GOUNOD: Aimons-nous; Où voulez-vous aller?
SCHUBERT: Aufenthalt; Das Fischermädchen; Ihr Bild; In der Ferne
SCHUMANN, Robert: Lust der Sturmnacht; Mein schöner Stern; Stille Liebe;
   Stille Tränen; Widmung
      Gérard Souzay, bar; Dalton Baldwin, pf

60320. *The Art of Elisabeth Schumann*
BACH: Bist du bei mir
BRAHMS: Nachtigall
HANDEL: O Had I Jubal's Lyre
MAHLER: Wer hat dies Liedlein erdacht?
MENDELSSOHN: Auf Flügeln des Gesanges
MOZART: Alleluia; L'Amero sara costante
REGER: Maria Wiegenlied
SCHUBERT: Der Hirt auf dem Felsen
SMETANA: Cradle Song
ZELLER: Sei nicht bös; Wie mein Ahn'l zwanzig Jahr
    Elisabeth Schumann, sop; Reginald Kell, cl; George Reeves, pf,
    instruments

SPECTRUM

SR-147. *Songs of Lex Six*
AURIC: Alphabet
DUREY: Songs from Le Bestiaire de Apollinaire
HONEGGER: Six Poèmes de Apollinaire
MILHAUD: Chansons de poèmes juifs
POULENC: Air romantique; Air vif; A sa guitare; Il vole; Souric et mouric
TAILLEFERRE: Six Chansons françaises
    Maria Lagios, sop; Elizabeth Buccheri, pf

TELEFUNKEN

6,42350 AW. *Lieder*
DALLAPICCOLA: Sieben Goethe-Lieder
SCHOENBERG: Herzgewächse
STRAVINSKY: Elegy for J. F. K.; Three Songs from William Shakespeare
WEBERN: Drei Lieder; Drei Volktexte; Fünf geistliche Lieder; Fünf Kanons
   nach lateinischen Texten; Sechs Lieder nach Gedichten von Georg Trakl
    Dorothy Dorow, sop; Ensemble Amsterdam, de Leeuw

642620. *Ballads*
  LOEWE: Graf Eberstein; Harald
  SCHUBERT: Erlkönig; Loda's Gespenst; Der Zwerg
  SCHUMANN, Robert: Die beiden Grenadiere; Belsatzar; Die feindlichen
    Brüder; Der Soldat; Die wandelnde Glocke
      Werner Hollweg, ten; Roman Ortner, pf

UNICORN
  RHS 369. *Songs of Herbert Howells and C. W. Orr*
    HOWELLS: Alas Alack; Come Sing and Dance; The Dunce; King David; The
      Lady Caroline; Merry Margaret; Miss T; On the Merry First of May; The
      Three Cherry Trees
    ORR: Along the Field; Bahnhofstrasse; Farewell to Barn and Stack and
      Tree; In Valleys Green and Still; Is My Team Ploughing; The Lads in
      Their Hundreds; When I Watch the Living Meet; When Smoke Stood Up
      from Ludlow; While Summer On Is Stealing; With Rue My Heart Is Laden
        Philip Langridge, ten; Bruce Ogston, bar; Eric Parkin, pf

SECTION **3** *Title/First Line Index*

Title/First Line Index